Nathalie Pré

TORONTO
URBAN
STROLLS ②
... for girlfriends

The girlfriends-tested guide
to exciting walks in Toronto

Word
— of —
Mouth
Production

This book is dedicated to my girlfriends.
"Don't walk behind me; I may not lead. Don't walk in front of me;
I may not follow. Just walk beside me and be my friend."
– Albert Camus

Copyright © 2013 by Word-of-Mouth Production
All rights reserved. No portion of this book may be reproduced
in any form without written permission from the publisher.

Published by Word-of-Mouth Production
299 Booth Avenue
Toronto, Ontario M4M 2M7, Canada
Tel.: (416) 462-0670
mail@torontofunplaces.com

Follow the author on:

torontourbanstrolls.com
torontofunplaces.com
twitter.com/NathaliePrezeau
pinterest.com/NathaliePrezeau

Writing and photos: **Nathalie Prézeau**
Illustrations: **Johanne Pepin**
Proofreading: **Kerstin McCutcheon**
Honorary members of the author's exclusive Friends Whom I Exploit Shamelessly Club:
**François Bergeron, Christian Castel, Claire Marier, Kerstin & Ryan McCutcheon,
Maude Prézeau, Anne-Frédéric Laurin**

Design and layout: **Publisher Friendly Inc.** (416) 462-0670
Printing: **Marquis Book Printing Inc.** (418) 246-5666

Library and Archives Canada Cataloguing in Publication

Prézeau, Nathalie, 1960 –
    Toronto urban strolls 2: –for girlfriends : the girlfriends-tested guide to exciting walks in
    Toronto / Nathalie Prézeau.
Includes index.
ISBN 978-0-9684432-8-6

1. Toronto (Ont.) – Tours.
2. Walking – Ontario – Toronto – Guidebooks. I. Title. II. Title: Toronto urban strolls two.

FC3097.18.P76 2013   917.13'541045   C2013-901633-3

A word from the author

When I first decided to write a walking guide for girlfriends (and guys man enough to handle a guide for women), I had a feeling that we were all ready to enjoy more simple pleasures (the kind that don't deplete wallets or energy). Well, I won my bet!

Last summer, 5,000 copies of **Toronto Urban Strolls... for girlfriends 1** sold out in three months and my guide made the *Globe and Mail*'s bestsellers list in the Canadian Non-fiction category. It is now available in its second edition, with 28 updated walks.

Girlfriends of all ages told me they had done a couple of strolls together and were already planning their next walk. Young retirees were excited to have so many urban sights to explore. Many business owners said they had customers coming to their store for the first time, with my book in hand. Locals couldn't believe there was still so much for them to discover. Tourists were thrilled with the guarantee they would find the cool little spots their crowd usually misses. And my own girlfriends saw how a little change of scenery can do wonders to recharge their batteries.

Toronto Urban Strolls... for girlfriends 2 offers 24 new strolls to help us feel the joy that comes in ordinary moments, when we walk, talk, see, stop, sit, eat, shop, chat, stroll, watch, sip and laugh... with our friends.

My TOP-3 reasons for loving to walk?
It is the best way to discover a city. It's the most fun way to stay in shape. And I know from experience that great walks in good company lead to great talks.

Enjoy!

Nathalie Prézeau

Author, publisher, photographer
mail@torontofunplaces.com

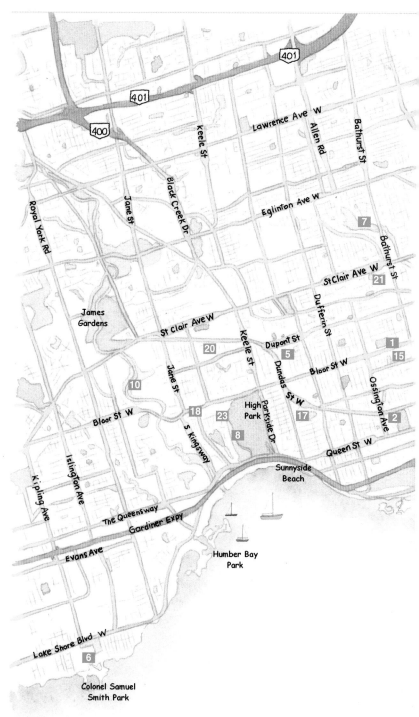

TORONTO URBAN STROLLS MAP

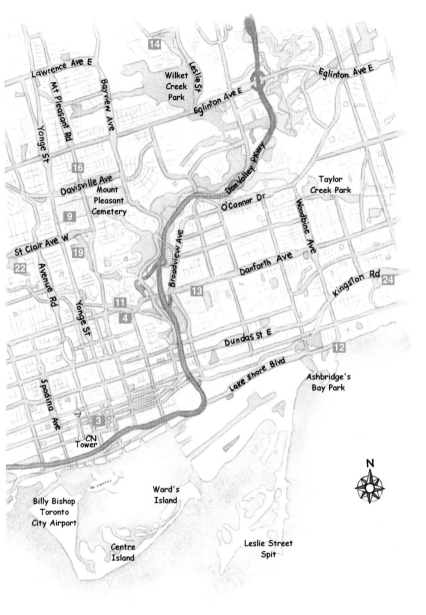

Legend:

1 to **24** = Reference to stroll number
in the guide

Table of Contents

I SPY
STROLLS

NATURE
STROLLS

NEIGHBOURHOOD STROLLS

STAMINA BUILDING STROLLS

There's **28 more** themed walks in **Toronto Urban Strolls 1**

Did you really think the author would have left out Cabbagetown, Liberty Village, Kensington Market, Ward's Island and the likes? No way!

BLOOR WEST
COOL STROLL

1

A really cool stroll, honest!

Bordering the **University of Toronto** and **Koreatown**, this walk is filled with student-friendly stores, restaurants and venues. You can hunt down unique finds in the vintage, second-hand or one-of-a-kind shops. It includes great murals to be seen in the lanes, charming houses to be admired off Bloor Street West, as well as iconic **Honest Ed's**, frozen in time. This is the stroll for cult film buffs, avid readers and music lovers, amateurs of exotic food experiences, collectors of comic books and board games. Come to think about it, if you're a fan of the TV show *The Big Bang Theory*, this one is for you.

STROLL

1

Full loop:
4.4 km (1 hr 05 min)

Shorter version:
If you stick to the part
of the stroll east of
Snakes and Lattes on
Bloor, you'll still get to
see most Bloor West
cool features in a
2.8 km stroll (40 min).

Game for more?
Harbord Village
Dolce Vita Stroll
(**Stroll 15**, p. 93)
touches Grace Street,
just south of Bloor W.

Parking & TTC
• Exit at **Bathurst**,
Christie or **Spadina**
Subway Stations.
• It's easier to find free
street parking north
of Bloor (try around
Howland or Albany).
There's a **Green P** on
Lippincott, south of
Bloor W.

Other TIPS
• For the listing of films
shown at **The Bloor**
Hot Doc Cinema (506
Bloor W.) visit
bloorcinema.com.
• **Snakes & Lattes**
(600 Bloor W.) is a
board game café/
store where you get
to choose from over
2,000 games to play,
for a small fee.

Bloor Street West

I usually find free parking
spots north of Bloor when
driving along Howland,
Wells and Albany. When I
have no luck, I keep driving south of Bloor, where
Albany becomes Lippin-
cott and there's a **Green P**
(on the east side).

I was told **Hey Lucy**
at 440 Bloor W. is a
good place for a bite or
drink with the girls. Maybe
on your way back? Nearby
Outer Layer (430 Bloor W.)
is filled with trinkets, cards
and gadgets.

Many other stores
contribute to the cool vibe
of this part of Bloor, such
as **Inti Crafts**, just west of
Howland (carrying lots of
original clothes), **Grass-**
roots and their environ-
mental products (408 Bloor
W.) or **Book City** across
the street (expect a fun
assortment of books in the
front).

Future Bistro further
east (483 Bloor W.) is an
Annex institution.

From the look of it, you
wouldn't know it but
BMB (471 Bloor W.) sells
new and used books over
three vast floors. You'll pay
a third of the regular price.

Across the street,
The Labyrinth Store (386
Bloor W.) carries a fantastic selection of books on
animation, graffiti, Manga,
how-to books and more.

Major Street

Walk south on Major
Street for a glimpse of
this charming neighbour-
hood. (The houses at Major
and Sussex really have
character.)

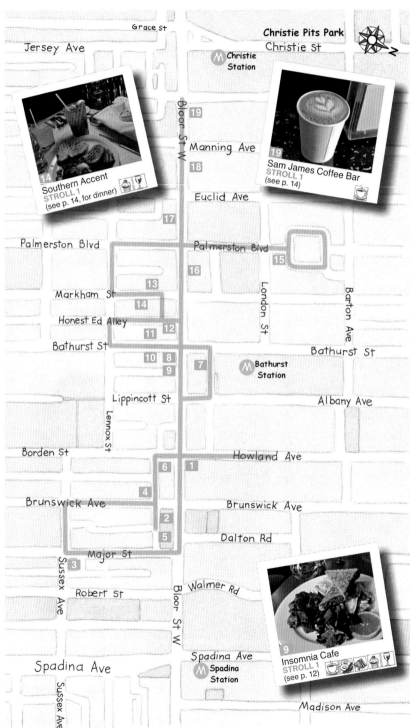

Grace St

Jersey Ave

Christie Pits Park

Christie St

M Christie Station

Bloor St W

19

Manning Ave

18

14 Southern Accent
STROLL 1
(see p. 14, for dinner)

19 Sam James Coffee Bar
STROLL 1
(see p. 14)

Euclid Ave

17

Palmerston Blvd

Palmerston Blvd

15

16

London St

Barton Ave

Markham St

13

14

Honest Ed Alley

11 **12**

Bathurst St

10 **8**

9

7

M Bathurst Station

Bathurst St

Lippincott St

Albany Ave

Lennox St

Borden St

Howland Ave

6 **1**

4

Brunswick Ave

Brunswick Ave

2

5

Dalton Rd

Major St

Sussex Ave

3

Robert St

Bloor St W

Walmer Rd

9 Insomnia Cafe
STROLL 1
(see p. 12)

Spadina Ave

M Spadina Station

Spadina Ave

Sussex Ave

Madison Ave

Turn west on Sussex, then north on Brunswick Avenue to access the lane right before Bloor, where you'll find a great cluster of ambitious murals.

Tranzac Club

4 You can't miss the funky mural on the lane side of **Tranzac Club** (292 Brunswick).

5 I recommend you first walk into the lane east of Brunswick. That's where I found a painted woman, a masterpiece in spray paint art.

6 Then, follow the lane westbound, past the **Tranzac Club**. Beyond the groovy entrance to the **Green Room** is an impressive artwork reminiscent of the psychedelic era.

Turn right on Borden Street, then left on Bloor.

Lippincott Street

A bit further west on the north side, check the urban decor of **Aroma Espresso Bar** at Lippincott.

7 Then take Lippincott north and turn left into the first lane, by little **Seaton Park** for a music-themed mural.

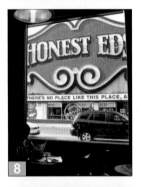

Bathurst Street

8 Walking southbound on Bathurst you'll find **Green Beanery**, a coffee place with a view over iconic **Honest Ed's**.

9 Before going south, we had a delicious breakfast served by an upbeat waiter at **Insomnia**, east of Bathurst (563 Bloor W., open daily for breakfast, at least from 10 a.m.).

10 We enjoyed our visit to clothing and accessories store **Trove** (791 Bathurst).

11 Then we entered über cool **Sonic Boom** (across the street), packed with music finds.

Honest Ed Alley

12 Walking further south on Bathurst, turn right at Lennox Street, then right again into Honest Ed Alley to see some interesting murals. Then turn right on Bloor for a unique Toronto experience: getting lost in the run-down labyrinth of bargain centre **Honest Ed's** (581 Bloor W.).

It belongs to the same people who own the Mirvish theatres, hence the huge posters and autographed photos of showbiz stars all over the place.

Markham Street

13 The western exit of the store (if you can find your way out!) opens into **Mirvish Village**, hosting an eclectic collection of one-of-a-kind shops.

Competing for the attention of movie buffs: **Vintage Video** (a huge store) and **Hollywood Canteen**, both selling movies, posters and movie memorabilia, and **Suspect Video & Culture** across the street (605 Markham), specializing in horror movies).

Nearby **Beguiling** is the best store in town to buy comic books (601 Markham).

Every little store on Markham is surprising but if you're a fashion lover don't miss **Casa Como** at

606 Markham (they carry wild creations of up-and-coming creators).

14 In the gorgeous decor of **Coal Miner's Daughter** (587 Markham), the boutique co-owner will probably be busy at her sewing machine.

EweKnit is a yarn supplier next door offering workshops... and coffee (there's a cute nook with tables by the windows).

Southern Accent (595 Markham) is my favourite restaurant on the street (opens at 5 p.m., closed on Mondays). They have a psychic in-house!

Victory Café has the perfect patio for a late afternoon summer drink.

Palmerston Square

Turn right at Lennox, then right again onto Palmerston (these houses are something, aren't they?).

15 Past Bloor, it will lead you to Palmerston Square, a quaint little loop worth the detour.

16 **Snakes & Lattes** board game café is just east at 600 Bloor West.

Koreatown

17 Among the interesting finds along **Koreatown** (westbound to Christie), I noticed beautiful rubber stamp kits at **Hanji** (619 Bloor W.).

18 Walnut-shaped cakes and thick pancakes at **Hodo Kwaja** at 656, and exotic grocery items at **P.A.T. Central** (675).

19 Toronto's tiniest shop, **Sam James Coffee Bar**, is at 688a Bloor West.

A mix-and-match stroll

The appeal of **Ossington Village** is in the compound effect of all the whimsical details you'll observe on Ossington and Dundas West, on the street and inside the unique businesses: Cool signs, architectural features, street art, funky menus. You'll mistake a gym for a café and an office for a salon. The trendy mixes seamlessly with the old school, and I'm not just talking about tasteful vintage stores alternating with original designer shops. Here, it's classy Italian Sfingi balls versus good old Portuguese custard pies, dark pubs against bright hipster restaurants, fancy art galleries contrasting with graffiti-filled lanes...

STROLL 2

Full loop:
3.9 km (1 hr)

Shorter version:
Skip the walk in the park and the stroll drops to 2.9 km (45 min).

Game for more?
Harbord VIllage Dolce Vita Stroll (Stroll 15, p. 93) is less than a 10 min walk north of this stroll.

Parking & TTC
• The streetcar **#505** runs along Dundas West and streetcar **#501** rides along Queen West.
• There's a small **Green P** lot east of Ossington at 1117 Dundas W.

Other TIPS
• **Lower Ossington Theatre** (**LOT**) is a 147-seat theatre with a penchant for musicals (the kind of place where you could catch a live *Rocky Horror Show* on Halloween). It is located at 100A Ossington, between Argyle and Humbert Streets. (The **Green Door Cabaret** in the same building has tables with bar service.)

A good plan

The best way to enjoy this stroll is to start it mid-afternoon on a warm day. You get to see the surroundings and catch a few stores before their closing. Then, late afternoon drink at one of the patios, followed by dinner at another place.

On your way out, it will be dark and you'll get to do a night walk to admire the lights within the restaurants and the little lounges oozing a cool vibe along Ossington. How is that for a plan?

Lakeview Avenue

1 I suggest you try to park along or near quiet Lakeview Avenue. It is lovely with the grassy borders by the sidewalk on both sides and lined with quaint houses.

2 It meets Churchill Avenue northbound (the cutest street, hilly and curvy, with the **CN Tower** pointing over the roofs). Then walk southbound on Ossington to Dundas West.

Little Portugal

3 It becomes obvious that you're in **Little Portugal** when you explore Dundas west of Ossington.

When you stand at the corner of Lakeview Avenue and Dundas West, you see Portugal's national black rooster painted on a wall. Two Portuguese bakeries face each other.

Left and right of **Caldense Bakery** (1298 Dundas W.) there's a churrasqueira, an escola de conduçâo and an agencia portuguesa de viagens.

Bellwoods Brewery
STROLL 2
(see p. 20)

Trinity
Bellwoods
Park

Pizzeria Libretto
STROLL 2
(see p. 19)

Ideal Coffee
STROLL 2
(see p. 19)

4 But most importantly, there's **Cristal Shoes Boutique** (1153 Dundas W.), carrying Helsar, the sophisticated line of shoes made in Portugal.

Dundas Street West

Penny Arcade (1177 Dundas W.) sells vintage clothes and so does **Bridge + Bardot**, some revamped with a modern touch (1138 Dundas W.).

5 You could stop for an all-day breakfast in retro **Lakeview Restaurant**, next door. (Your chance to try a deep fried Mars bar!)

6 Then, walk across Dundas and into the graffiti lane located right after **A1 Auto Service** further east on Dundas.

7 Turn left on Halton Street to reach the **Cathedral of the Nativity of the Mother of God** on Shaw Street. It is guarded by four white angels and features an impressive mosaic on the door.

Go across the parkette on the north side of the church to explore the Dundas stretch along **Trinity-Bellwoods Park**.

8 On the west side of Crawford Avenue, you'll find **The Tempered Press** (a casual café with a large window facing the park). On the east side, there's **Miracle Thieves** with a groovy mural on its Dundas facade. It promotes local artists, offers monthly workshops and pop-up shop events.

9 Further is **Armed**, a small boutique filled with unique fashion finds at 1024 Dundas West.

Le Dolci (1006 Dundas W.) sells yummy cupcakes and gives cupcake workshops in its elegant foodie studio.

10 Cross Dundas at Montrose Avenue to follow the path into **Trinity-Bellwoods Park**. (For a better view, keep to the higher trail, then cut down the stairs and keep going south.)

11 Turn right to reach Crawford Street and go northbound (aren't these houses lovely?).

12 Walk around the church on your left and return to Halton Street to admire the gorgeous Victorian mansion turned into **Maynard Nursing Home** (28 Halton), on your way to Ossington Avenue.

Ossington Avenue

13 The great sign of the tiny dark lounge **The Painted Lady (**218 Ossington) sets the tone, and **BQM** (with the giant burger/moon mural at Rolyat Avenue) adds to it.

14 We've had a pizza to die for (and Sfingi balls) at **Pizzeria Libretto**, across the street.

15 I loved the tasteful retro display of **Vintage Mix 1** (186 Ossington), tasted intriguing yummy soft boiled and then fried eggs at **Hawker Bar** (164) and had great coffee in welcoming **Ideal Coffee** (162).

16 Everything in **Phillip Sparks** (around the corner on Foxley), turned out to be beautifully crafted, down to the shoes made in Italy following his designs.

17 **Quasi Modo** is a fantastic furniture store right next to **Bellwoods Brewery** (124) our favourite spot to sit and watch people while sipping their Roman Candle beer!

18 We had a ball with the lively owners of designer shop **Studio Gang** (112A) and quality vintage **Rescue** (102).

We peeked into the **Lower Ossington Theatre** (100A) to see their cool chalk-paint wall.

We missed the gorgeous backyard patio of **Union** at 72 Ossington. (Note that there's a cute one in the back of coffee shop **Crafted** at 135.)

19 Further south, I was impressed by the bountiful selection of high-end vintage of **I Miss You** (63).

20 It faces the original gym/store/café **Academy of Lions** (64).

There's **Jonathan + Olivia** (49) a big airy store carrying new collections, and **Silver Falls Vintage** (15) with **Tusk** selling new clothes and never worn vintage in the back.

Around the corner at Queen sits the new high-end clothing store **Gravity-pope** (1010 Queen West).

21 In the first lane to your right past the store awaits a graffiti lane which gets more impressive the closer you get to Humbert Street. There's some serious artistry involved here!

22 Finally, look up to see the architectural detail on the **Levack** building at Humbert and Ossington.

Bohmer, the chic restaurant across the street, looks lovely in the evening.

PATH
UNDERGROUND STROLL

Save this stroll for rainy days

If you think the **PATH** is all about saving business people the trouble of putting a coat on when they go out for lunch, you might wonder what's in there for you? A lot, actually! The **PATH** connects over 50 buildings, office towers, food courts, shops and subway stations. Everywhere, we can pop out of the concourse level (not unlike groundhogs) to admire the wealth of indoor public art at street level in major downtown buildings. Expect bright and shiny corridors, great perspectives on intricate corporate architectural detail, noisy chaos on weekdays and church-like serenity on the weekends.

STROLL 3

Full loop:
5.7 km (1 hr 25 min)

Shorter version:
The stroll is 5 km (1 hr 15 min) if you drop **Air Canada Centre**.

Game for more?
The **Dundas Station** section and the art walk in **Toronto Dominion Centre** each add 1 km (15 min). **City Hall** adds .6 km (7 min).

Parking & TTC
• The **PATH** is connected to **Dundas**, **Queen**, **King**, **Union** and **St. Andrew Subway Stations**.
• **City Hall**'s indoor parking (110 Queen W., $14/weekdays, $6/weekends) connects to the **Sheraton Hotel**, which leads to **The Bay** eastbound.

Other TIPS
• See **torontopath.com** to print the official map.
• Note that most businesses along the PATH are closed on weekends!
• The **Design Exchange** (Canada's design museum) is in **Ernst & Young Tower** (234 Bay). Admission is $15, open every day. Visit **dx.org**.

The Hudson's Bay

1 The gorgeous **Foodwares Market** in the lower level of **The Bay** by **Queen Subway** exit (which includes a bigger section on the west side of the store), is the perfect starting point for this stroll. It opens at 7:30 a.m. on weekdays, later on weekends.

There are usually **PATH** signs hanging from the ceiling between the **Market** and **Starbucks** (to tell you where you are and where you're heading) but they were down at the time of print, due to renovations.

Walk east (towards the luggage section) to enter **One Queen East**.

One Queen East

2 Standing at the foot of the escalator in **One Queen Street East**, you'll see a splendid sculpture over your head, like a railway gone wild, and a wonderful painting.

Take the escalator down on your left. Walk through the subway station to access **2 Queen Street East**, where you'll find five limestone bas-relief.

Bay-Adelaide Centre

Returning to **The Bay**, turn left (south, then follow the alley on your right until you see an escalator going down to **Bay-Adelaide Centre** (on your left).

3 In that building, on weekdays, you'll see people in suits swarming the fancy food court and glossy corridors. (I loved the decor in the back of the **Marché**, and they serve wine!)

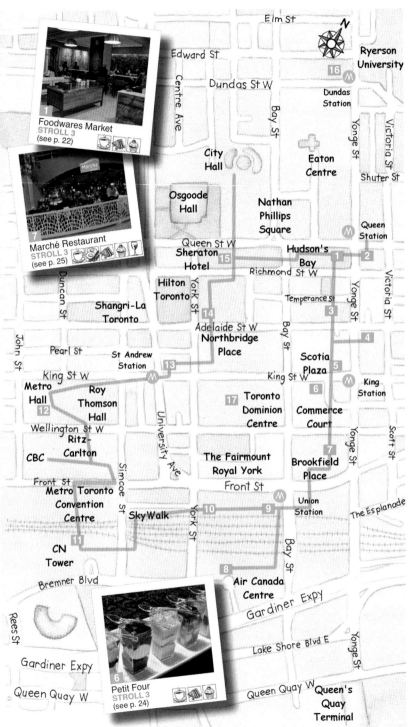

Foodwares Market
STROLL 3
(see p. 22)

Marché Restaurant
STROLL 3
(see p. 25)

Elm St

Edward St

Ryerson
University

16

Dundas St W

Dundas
Station

Centre Ave

Bay St

Yonge St

Victoria St

City
Hall

Eaton
Centre

Shuter St

Osgoode
Hall

Nathan
Phillips
Square

Queen
Station

Queen St W
Sheraton
Hotel   15

Hudson's
Bay

1   2

Richmond St W

Duncan St

York St

Hilton
Toronto

Temperance St

Yonge St

Victoria St

3

14

Shangri-La
Toronto

Adelaide St W
Northbridge
Place

Bay St

4

Scotia
Plaza

5

John St

Pearl St

St Andrew
Station

13

King St W

Scott St

King Station

King St W

6

Metro
Hall   12

Roy
Thomson
Hall

17

Toronto
Dominion
Centre

Commerce
Court

Wellington St W
Ritz-
Carlton

University Ave

Simcoe St

7

CBC

The Fairmount
Royal York

Brookfield
Place

Front St
Metro Toronto
Convention
Centre

Front St

Union
Station

The Esplanade

York St

SkyWalk   10

9

11

Bay St

CN
Tower

8

Bremner Blvd

Air Canada
Centre

Gardiner Expy

Rees St

Yonge St

Gardiner Expy

Lake Shore Blvd E

Queen Quay W

Petit Four
STROLL 3
(see p. 24)

Queen Quay W   Queen's
Quay
Terminal

Walk through **Scotia Plaza** doors on your left and, all of a sudden, you'll be in a world of red granite.

Scotia Plaza

You'll see the blond wood of **Ninki** restaurant on your right and **Winners** on your left (not open on weekends). Turn left and walk through the food court into **Dundee Place**.

4 Take the escalator up (on your left) to see the spectacular glass ceiling over the building's entrance.

5 Backtrack to **Winners**, turn left (south) and then right through the elevators. Then take the escalator to the street level to admire the breathtaking *Waterfall* painting by Derek Besant in **Scotiabank**.

Double back down the escalator and around to **Commerce Court** (left at **Second Cup**).

Commerce Court

6 You'll enter the classy corridor, with elaborate inlaid floor, of **Commerce Court**. Take the imposing staircase up (on your right past **Sloane** tea merchants).

Upstairs, you'll see elephants in the courtyard and Toronto's most beautiful ceiling inside **CIBC Private Wealth Management** (which you can enter on weekdays).

Back downstairs, turn right. On weekdays, walk to the end of **Commerce Court South** to grab a dessert shooter or a salad in a cup at **Petit Four**.

Then return to the circle at the centre of the **Court**.

Brookfield Place

7 Follow the signs to **BCE Place** (**Brookfield Place**'s former name). It turns right at **Hockey Hall of Fame**. Go up the central escalator for a splendid view of the six-storey arches.

Walk east around the escalator to see how the historic facade of **RBC Dominion Securities** was integrated in the modern architecture.

Further east before **Marché Restaurant** (which is perfect for a bite any day at any time), check the photo wall on your left in **Bay Wellington Tower**. Then, back down the central escalator to the end of the food court, past **McDonald's**, and turn left.

Air Canada Centre

Follow the signs to **Union Station** (but don't pay to enter the subway). This section is under construction and it will be tricky for a while. Find (or ask) your way to **GO Transit** (until renos are over you'll have to walk across an outdoor lane to get there).

Follow the signs to **Air Canada Centre**. In the back, you'll see a door to the **Centre** on the right.

Inside **Air Canada Centre**, turn right, then take the door to **25 York** on your right. (Check the tall poles pierced with stars in the square on your left!)

8 Past **Starbucks** awaits the amazing *Pixel Cube* by David Rokeby, its 30,000 LED lights dancing like northern lights.

For a real treat, enjoy a dessert under the sculptural lamps of beautiful **Aria Ristorante** on your left (closed on Sundays).

Retrace your steps to **GO Transit** and turn west to access the SkyWalk. (At the time of print I turned left at **Purdy's Chocolates** but the layout will eventually change.)

9 Taking the stairs up to **Union Station**, look up to view the impressive high ceiling of the historic train station, then follow the **SkyWalk** westbound.

The SkyWalk

10 Look up to see the **CN Tower** through the glass ceiling of the **SkyWalk**. A fun urban sight!

Turn left when you see the entrance sign to the **Metro Toronto Convention Centre**.

The escalator on your right will take you to the **South Building**, to see the giant turtle and other animals inlaid in the floor.

11 The escalator on your left leads to the **North Building** through a tunnel with pink glass windows.

Go down the two flights of stairs and walk westbound. On weekdays, you can exit into the street at **Second Cup** and enter **CBC**. On weekends, you take the first exit off the **Convention Centre** and follow the (covered) sidewalk on your right and cross to enter **Simcoe Place** (at the northwest corner of Front and Simcoe).

Follow the clearly indicated directions to **CBC Broadcast Centre** to see its spectacular glass ceiling up the stairs.

Metro Hall

Then double back, following the signs to **RBC Centre**. It will lead you through a long corridor adorned with interesting pixelated photos. Turn right at the **Ritz Carlton** and follow the signs for **Roy Thomson Hall** and **Metro Centre**.

12 At the food court, keep your left. Then take **Metro Hall** entrance on your left (facing **Reitmans**). On the other side of the wide doors is a great mural by fourteen high-school students.

Backtrack to **Reitmans** and turn left. Your next stop is the corridor along a pond (emptied in the winter), leading to **Roy Thomson Hall**.

Sun Life Centre

13 Through **St. Andrews Subway**, enter the **Sun Life Financial Tower**. See the fun interactive floor on your left? Up the escalator is my favourite spot to sit: the elegant sofas under the groovy lamps in **Sun Life Centre**.

On weekdays, from 7 a.m. to 4 p.m., you can grab a creamy latte at **SJCB** at the end of the long white corridor straight ahead before entering **Exchange Tower**.

130 Adelaide West

Follow the signs north (left) to **Richard Adelaide Complex**. Walk around the food court, turn left at **Northbridge Place** and left again at **Starbucks** to follow the **PATH** sign west to **150 York Street**. It leads to **130 Adelaide West.**

14 Take the escalator up to street level to admire the striking multimedia art on the **Oxford ARTablet**.

Then double back to **Starbucks** and go north (left) towards **Sheraton Centre Hotel**.

Sheraton Centre Hotel

15 Climb up the hotel lobby's escalator to admire the hotel's picturesque outdoor waterfall from the huge bay window.

Then return to the concourse level and follow signs to **Hudson's Bay Company**.

(To go to **City Hall** instead, turn north. Once in the parking lot, turn right and follow the yellow stripes on your left to a staircase taking you to **City Hall**'s rotunda.)

Want more art?

16 There's the terra cotta crowd by William McElcheran at the bottom and the top of the escalator to **Dundas Subway Station** (at the end of **Eaton Centre**). Look for the northbound train signs.

Toronto Dominion Centre is confusing (signs still using former names) but worth visiting to see all the art. Among other things, it includes **Ernst & Young Tower** (**Design Exchange** museum is up the escalator) and **95 Wellington West** with the *Flying* sculpture.

17 **TD South Tower** (TD Waterhouse Tower) features the **Gallery of Inuit Art** (in a mezzanine accessible at street level).

SHERBOURNE
HIGH & LOW MIX STROLL

4

A world of contrasts

Sherbourne Street is a part of town where fancy new high-rises face old condemned houses. Topped by high-brow **Rosedale** on the north and flanked by low-brow **St. James Town** on the east side, it's hard to find one single word to describe its essence. Walking through secluded **Wellesley-Magill Park** then strolling along the lively path of the public place near **Food Basics** are two totally different experiences. The stroll includes the beautiful green houses of **Allan Gardens Conservatory** and a peek over the treetops along majestic Rosedale Valley Road.

STROLL 4

Full loop:
3.2 km (48 min)

Shorter version:
You'll find most of the interesting contrasts north of Wellesley. For a 2.1 km stroll (35 min), skip Homewood Ave., go east on Wellesley and continue the stroll at **Food Basics**.

Game for more?
Rosedale Valley Fall Colours Stroll
(**Stroll 11**, p. 69) is accessible from the staircase at the northwest corner of Bloor and Mount Pleasant, a 5-min. walk away.

Parking & TTC
• Exit at **Sherbourne Subway Station**.
• There's a **Green P** lot north of Carlton at 405 Sherbourne.

Other TIPS
• At the time of print, a major condo project was on its way between Sherbourne and Glen Road. It might affect access to the pedestrian bridge over Rosedale Valley.
• Admission to **Allan Gardens Conservatory** is free. It is open daily from 10 a.m. to 5 p.m.

Bleecker Street

Street parking is a bit tricky to find in the area so I recommend the **Green P** parking lot at 405 Sherbourne (north of Carlton).

1 Start north of Carlton on Bleecker Street (accessible off the east side of the parking lot if you've parked there) to see the cutest little trompe-l'oeil on the back of long-term care **Fudger House** (it faces the small park you'll see on your right).

Cross the street and walk east on Wellesley until you reach the grocery store **Food Basics**.

2 On your way, you can't miss the giant hand painting a huge wolf on the side of a variety store. (It is part of a **City Art Project** initiative.)

3 Walk around this building and you'll see another original artwork from the same project: two mesmerizing eyes about to stare at you.

St. James Town

In the summer, this part of town is unique. The paved path running north into **St. James Town** becomes lively with all the high-rise residents enjoying the nice weather. The air is filled with the joyful cry of kids playing in the high-rise's outdoor pool. Mothers chat while keeping an eye on their children in the playgrounds.

4 Others are strolling along the path and browsing through items for sale on the grass.

5 There's more art on structures and walls.

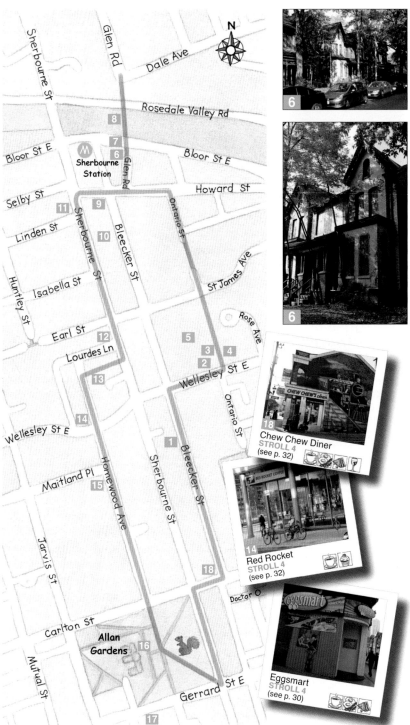

Chew Chew Diner
STROLL 4
(see p. 32)

Red Rocket
STROLL 4
(see p. 32)

Eggsmart
STROLL 4
(see p. 30)

Keep walking north on the path and you'll pass by **Rose Avenue Public School** where I noticed a pretty mosaic in a reflecting pool (empty in the fall). Further north you'll reach Howard Street.

Howard Street

Howard Street and Glen Road seemed frozen in time during my visit. The great houses from 1889 on Glen were condemned and this nook looked like a ghost town, but they will get a major makeover when the construction of a large development starts.

6 The City's Community Planning office confirmed the houses' facades are to be retained.

7 An entrance to **Sherbourne Subway Station** is located at the foot of Glen, right next to a tunnel running under Bloor Street.

8 Go through this tunnel to get to the pedestrian bridge. It will offer you a wonderful view over Rosedale Valley Road, at its best in the fall. You're now in the affluent neighbourhood of Rosedale.

9 Back on Glen, turn right on Howard to reach Sherbourne.

10 You might want to have a peek into **St. James Town West Park** on your left. The large mural on its southern part celebrates *Article 26* in the **United Nations Declaration of Human Rights** (about everyone having the right to education).

Eggsmart serves hardy all-day breakfasts at 601 Sherbourne.

Sherbourne Street

11 **James Cooper House**, at the northwest corner of Sherbourne and Linden, is a beauty, built in the Second Empire style in 1881... 60 feet away from its current location!

When you look up to admire its mansard roof on the southern side, you'll see the most surprising section of *Inversion* (the conceptual bronze sculptures of life-size animals by Eldon Garnet). More animals await by the front door.

12 Further south is another landmark: **Our Lady of Lourdes Church** at 520 Sherbourne, noticeable for its dome contrasting against a background of modern buildings.

The bronze statue represents Bernadette, the young French woman (endorsed by the Catholic Church), who claims the Virgin Mary appeared to her 18 times in 1858.

13 Take the narrow path between the two towers (500 Sherbourne) to access an intriguing urban park: **Wellesley-Magill Park**. Instead of grass, it is covered with pebbles and some large polished rocks reflecting the surrounding buildings.

This secluded park hosts *Forest Walk*, a 144-foot long steel wall of intricate cutout work by artist Ed Pien.

Each panel has its own charm and when the sun shines through it at the right angle, it casts a lace pattern on the ground.

Homewood Avenue

14 You'll find hipster **Red Rocket Coffee** at the corner of Homewood and Wellesley.

Keep walking south-bound on Homewood until you reach **Allan Gardens** on Carlton Street.

15 Homeland Avenue is especially pretty around Maitland Place, where you'll see a lovely ivy-covered house. Further south on the opposite side is a rare sight in Toronto: two B & Bs, side by side (**Banting House Inn** at 73 Homewood, and quaint **Homewood Inn** at 65).

Allan Gardens

16 When you reach **Allan Gardens**, you're greeted by a giant green dog watching over the big dogs in the off-leash park. (A big blue dog overlooks the adjacent park for smaller pets.)

The six greenhouses offer an oasis in the middle of the city. The light! The smell! The colours! Quite the urban treat.

17 If you're with your girlfriends, you might muster enough courage to visit colourful **Take a Walk on the Wild Side**, a cross-dresser boutique, facing the park on Gerrard.

18 Back on Sherbourne, turn left and walk east on Carlton to **Chew Chew Diner** at Bleecker Street, admiring three churches along the way.

This restaurant, where I had good Eggs Benedict, offers a nice finish to the stroll and one last point of interest with its great mural.

Street art all around the block

Looking for street art in a big city feels a bit like a treasure hunt. One casually strolls around a neighbourhood, walks around the corner, and BAM! You're hit by the colourful sight of a huge mural splashed all over an unassuming wall. The **Junction Triangle** area hosts one of the best clusters in town for such surprises. Not to be confused with **The Junction**, sitting along Dundas West, west of Keele (see Stroll 20 on page 123), the **Junction Triangle** can actually be seen on any map. Formed by the junction of three railways, it runs through Dupont, Bloor and Dundas.

STROLL
5

Full loop:
7.2 km (1 hr 45 min)

Shorter version:
If you don't do the
sections north of
Dupont and south of
Bloor, the stroll will
drop to 5 km (1 hr 15
min).

Game for more?
You're such a keener!
**High Park Cherry
Blossom Stroll**
(Stroll 8, p. 51) is less
than 1 km west of this
stroll on Bloor. (It is
interesting even when
the cherry trees are
not in bloom.)

Parking & TTC
• Exit at **Lansdowne
and Dundas West
Subway Stations**.
• I usually find free
street parking along
Wallace Avenue or
nearby streets.

Other TIPS
• **Open Doors Design**
is Toronto's best pup-
pet shop and part of
the **Toronto Puppetry
Collective** producing
puppet shows through
Puppet Allsorts! in
Zuke Studio (1581
Dupont, with entrance
from the back alley off
Franklin Avenue). See
puppetallsorts.com.

Wallace Avenue

My favourite way to start
this stroll is with a walk
along the **West Toronto
Railpath** (a 2-km urban
trail built in 2009 along the
railway used by the GO-
Train).

1 I like to park around
Wallace Avenue and
grab a coffee at **Cafe
Neon** (a café with an artsy
industrial look serving light
lunches) before heading
northbound on the **West
Toronto Railpath** from the
Wallace entrance.

Each street it crosses
is marked with an angular
sculpture and the street's
first three letters cut out in
a metal sign.

2 The path runs up to
Cariboo Avenue, .8
km further north. Walking
straight to the end, you
can't miss (assuming it's
not been painted over) the
fish mural on the back of
the **Osler Fish Warehouse**
past Dupont.

3 It is followed by a
small hill offering a
surprising country feeling
to this part of town.

Further, check the
wire fence to your left, with
all the pieces of trees still
caught in the links. Nature
is strong!

Cariboo Avenue

By Cariboo entrance, you'll
find a full map of the urban
trail. The linear park ends
southbound at Dundas
West, 2.2 km from Cariboo.

4 Heading back south-
bound, stop on the
railpath (where it runs over
Dupont Street) to enjoy the
youthful mural on the north
side of Dupont.

Pelham Ave

Cariboo Ave

Osler St

Hugo Ave

Dupont St

Edwin Ave

Franklin Ave

Ruskin Ave

Kenneth Ave

Dundas St W

Jerome St W

Perth Ave

Symington Ave

Campbell Ave

Lansdowne Ave

Brandon Ave

Dupont St

Café Neon
STROLL 5
(see p. 34)

Wallace Ave

Glenlake Ave

Dorval Rd

Campbell Ave

Lansdowne Ave

Wallace Ave

Emerson Ave

Brock Ave

Edna Ave

Dundas St W

Ⓜ Lansdowne
Station

Alhambra Ave

Bloor St W

Bloor St W

St Helens Ave

St Clarens Ave

Marguerreta St

Brock Ave

Roncesvalles

Dundas St W

Golden Ave

Sorauren Ave

Lansdowne Ave

College St

Dundas St W

Starving Artist
STROLL 5
(see p. 38)

Zocalo
STROLL 5
(see p. 38)

Dupont Street

5 Go down the stairs to street level to take in the long bike-theme mural under the viaduct on the south side (it was funded by the City's Graffiti Transformation Project).

The mural features a lineup of life-size cyclists riding towards a huge pile of retired tires. Impressive!

Edwin Avenue

6 Walk east on Dupont to Edwin Avenue, where you'll notice the funky flank of **Farmhouse Tavern** self-described as "a blackboard menu of farm driven food". (Not open for lunch but they have a brunch on weekends from 11 a.m.)

7 After admiring the shiny roof of the **Ukrainian Orthodox Church of St. Andrew** across from the restaurant, head down Edwin Avenue for a real treat.

8 At the corner of Edwin and Clark Crescent, you'll find **Metropolis Factory**. That's where they make or recycle the original vintage stuff we see in **Metropolis Living** in **The Junction** (see p. 127).

You can roam freely in this cool industrial place open to the public, where they display the pieces too large to be displayed in their other store on Dundas West.

Back on Dupont

Turn left on Ruskin around the corner, then left again on Franklin Avenue to Dupont, where you'll turn right.

9 On your way to the next mural, you'll have a chance to sneak into **Open Door Designs** (1597 Dupont), the best place to buy vintage or new puppets. (They're the creators of a puppet theatre you hang in a doorway.)

Rose Antiques (1586 Dupont) is another place jam-packed with great vintage finds, from small objects to serious pieces of furniture.

Campbell Avenue

10 Keep walking just past Campbell Avenue and you won't be disappointed. You'll come across the captivating mural of Joel Richardson under the viaduct.

Believe it or not, this mural, first commissioned by the City of Toronto, was painted over following the war on graffiti by newly elected Rob Ford. The artist subsequently got the right to paint it back!

Take Campbell down to get back to Wallace where you'll turn left to get to Lansdowne, past the pretty railway crossroad.

Lansdowne Ave.

There's a little Portuguese pocket at the corner of Wallace and Lansdowne. Despite the name, the **Paris Bakery** carries Portuguese pastries including yummy custard tarts.

11 Then there's **O Bair-radino** (662 Lansdowne), a restaurant serving tasty and affordable Portuguese BBQ chicken. The perfect stop after the stroll to grab some take-out.

12 Walking south-bound, you'll see the lovely *Lansdowne Fence Streetscape* commissioned in 2010 by the TTC to temporarily mask a sad-looking vacant lot. (Let's hope we can enjoy it for a little while.) The delicate artwork covers the fences on two sides of the lot.

13 Across the street at Paton awaits **Starving Artist** (584 Lansdowne), a waffle and espresso bar where great waffles are served all day and the coffee is excellent.

There's also **Wallace Espresso** (188 Wallace at Lansdowne) and **Whippoorwill Tavern** (1285 Bloor West), a new diner offering brunch Friday to Sunday.

Bloor Street West

14 Turn right on Bloor and you'll be able to admire another intricate example of street art: a subtle series of elegant lace-like paintings.

15 Closer to the Bloor entrance to the Railpath is cool café **GT BT,** serving great empanadas (1421 Bloor W.). For a memorable (and affordable) lunch, you have to go to **Zocalo** across the street (open daily from 10 a.m.).

Dundas West

Climb up the stairs by the next viaduct on Bloor to return to the **Railpath**.

16 You can walk southbound to see the rest of the urban trail (Dundas West is 10 minutes away).

17 Or return to your starting point on Wallace.

For a glistening stroll

From Lake Shore Boulevard, you would not guess all the beauties lying ahead. **Colonel Samuel Smith Park** is one of Toronto's best kept secrets (which Etobicoke's locals have know all along, of course). Its waterfront park made from lake fill, has been so well naturalized that it has become a popular birding destination, a quiet oasis with pebble beaches, tall grass, ponds and enough trees for a great fall walk. It includes a lovely figure-8-shaped skating trail by a tall chimney and the **Humber College** campus, installed in Victorian buildings which used to be a psychiatric hospital.

STROLL 6

Full loop:
7 km (1 hr 45 min)

Shorter version:
The nature part of the stroll, not including Colonel Sam Smith Park Drive, is 5 km long (1 hr 15). And if you cut off the north-east branch leading out of the park, it's less than 1 hr long (3.8 km).

Game for more?
Keep walking west at the marina and take Lake Promenade, west of 23rd Street. Lake Promenade is a pretty 2 km road ending at **Marie Curtis Park** and passing by two other waterfront parks, **Long Branch** and **Len Ford**.

Parking & TTC
• The streetcar **#501** runs along Lake Shore Boulevard.
• Parking is free in the lot on your left at the end of the road (free on the weekend in the larger lot on your left, near the chimney).

Other TIPS
• **Colonel Sam Smith Skating Trail** opens daily from end of November to mid-March, 9 a.m. to 10 p.m.

Into the park
At the foot of Kipling Avenue on Lake Shore Blvd. West, is Colonel Samuel Smith Park Drive, passing through **Humber College** campus and taking you into the park.

If you want to grab a coffee, stop at the **Tim Hortons** you'll see on your left before the turn of the road.

1 Drive to the last parking lot you'll see on your left (always free). It's the closest to the waterfront trails in **Colonel Samuel Smith Park**.

I prefer to start the walk past the roundabout, taking the first trail on the right, and then turn right towards the marina.

At the marina
2 In the summer, there can be up to 150 boats moored in the sheltered little marina.

In the fall, there's enough trees around to make it look lovely.

If you were to keep going west, you'd reach Twenty Third Street, and the start of Lake Promenade. (This nice waterfront road lined with many quaint houses eventually takes you to the entrance of **Marie Curtis Park**, at Forty Second Street.)

Cn Tower in sight
3 Return to the paved circle and turn right, and right again on the main path. Then walk straight towards the lake, to the tip of the land stretching into **Lake Ontario**.

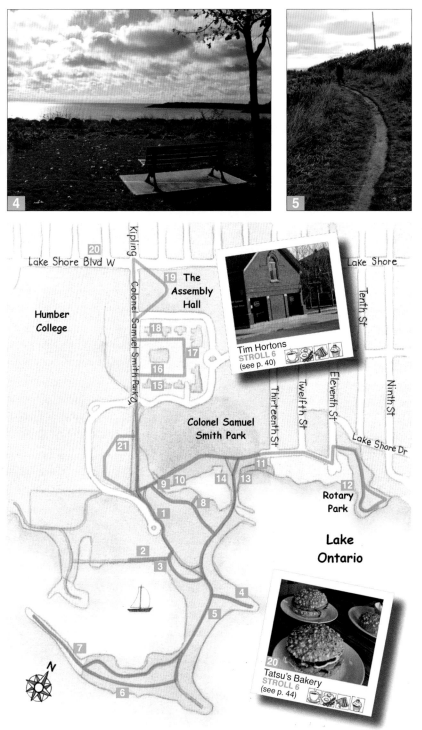

Tim Hortons
STROLL 6
(see p. 40)

Kipling

Lake Shore Blvd W

Colonel Samuel Smith Park Dr

Humber
College

The
Assembly
Hall

Lake Shore

Tenth St

18

17

16

15

Thirteenth St

Twelfth St

Eleventh St

Ninth St

Colonel Samuel
Smith Park

21

Lake Shore Dr

9 10   14 13

11

8

1

12

Rotary
Park

2

3

Lake
Ontario

4

5

7

N

6

Tatsu's Bakery
STROLL 6
(see p. 44)

4 On a bright day, you can clearly see the **CN Tower**, 11 km away.

A few benches along the path allow you to admire the panorama.

Southwest loop

5 Back on the main path, turn left to stroll up to the tip of the narrow break wall protecting the marina.

6 Some side trails take you closer to the water. That's where you'll get the widest panorama embracing the lake, especially gorgeous when glistening under the sun.

7 On your way back, take the left fork overlooking the marina. It will take you to the main path.

Walk eastbound, follow the curve left, then turn eastbound along the waterfront trail.

Around the pond

You could stay on the shoreline to reach the eastern end of the park but I suggest you explore the inner grounds of the park before.

8 Take the first path to your left then turn into the first clearing you notice on your right. It will take you to an observation deck overlooking the pond.

Then, follow the trail on the right amidst tall grass.

9 Walk around the parking lot and turn right to get to a very different environment of mature trees and green grass.

10 You'll eventually walk by a lovely cottage-like pavilion overlooking the pond.

11 You can then take the right towards the pebble beach or keep going east, out of the park to **Rotary Park**, .6 km further east.

Rotary Park

Follow Lakeshore Drive, past Thirteenth Street. At Eleventh Street, make a short turn left then walk through the green space with playground.

You'll see a path turning towards the lake. It leads to **Rotary Park**.

12 I thought the viewpoint of the shore in the little bay on the west side of the park was picture-perfect (with a team of ducks as a bonus).

The benches on the grassy part of the park offer the perfect break to admire the view.

13 Back into **Colonel Samuel Smith Park**, take the left fork towards the lake, for a chance to admire white swans by the pebble beach.

14 You'll see the pond amidst great wetlands on your right.

Take the trail on your right and keep walking until you reach the main path, where you'll turn left. Then turn right, through the grove, for yet another different view of the big park.

Humber College

15 Once you get to Colonel Samuel Smith Park Drive, you're entering **Humber College** campus, where the new mixes beautifully with gorgeous Victorian red brick buildings.

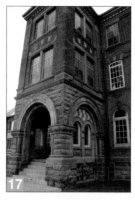

They used to belong to **Lakeshore Psychiatric Hospital** (which opened in 1889 and closed in 1979).

16 Stroll along the red brick road to have a better look at the architecture. (You can enter any of them.)

17 Look carefully and you'll notice something odd about one of them. Doors and windows are trompe-l'oeil which were painted on the condemned building (until **Humber College** gets the budget to renovate it).

18 Turn right along the drive and around the edifices to have a look at the impressive facades.

Then get closer to century-old **Assembly Hall** (a multi-purpose community centre cleverly named **Ah!**) to see reptilian-like modern art serving as benches around the centre. They're part of *The Third Garden*, a public art project.

19 Look down as you walk through the landscaped section by Lake Shore Blvd. to admire the rest of this public art, cast-bronze texts telling the story of the patients in a very touching way.

20 **Tatsu's Bakery** (3180 Lake Shore W.) is my favourite place around for a bite. On weekends, you can expect **Humber**'s music students honing their jazz skills in one corner!

21 Backtracking to the parking lot, walk through the trees on your right, under the tall chimney to see where the figure-8-shaped skating trail is in the winter.

FOREST HILL
RAVINE STROLL

Forest Hill's natural beauty

The first time I came across the Spadina and Lonsdale intersection in **Forest Hill Village**, I was charmed by the quaint little shops and restaurants. When I discovered the gorgeous properties in this expensive neighbourhood, I was in awe. And finally, when I got to walk through the impressive valley of **Cedarvale Park**, I was hooked. This stroll covers it all. As a bonus, it offers a stop at **Type**, one of the cool bookstores in Toronto and it points you to one of the cutest bronze statues in the city. And the good news is **St. Clair West Subway Station** includes a north exit right off the park.

STROLL 7

Full loop:
4.5 km (1 hr 05 min)

Shorter version:
The return trail between the staircase of Glen Cedar Road (where the pedestrian bridge is) and Spadina, is 2.4 km (35 min).

Game for more?
Casa Loma Staircase Stroll (Stroll 22, p.135) is one block south of the St. Clair West Station exit at the foot of **Cedarvale Park** (a 10-min walk).

Parking & TTC
• Exit at **St. Clair West Subway Station** (use the Heath Street exit).
• I usually find free street parking on Strathearn Road east and west of Glen Cedar Road.

Other TIPS
• **Dutch Dreams** is a (very) whimsical and unique ice cream shop just a 15-min walk south of the bridge of Glen Cedar Road. Follow Claxton Blvd. past the roundabout, turn right on Kenwood Ave. and left on Vaughan Rd. (can't miss it at 78).

Glenayr Road

1 At the end of very quiet Glenayr Road is a pedestrian access to **Cedarvale Park**. (From Bathurst Street, turn east on Burton Road, then south on Glenayr Road.)

I really enjoy parking there since it allows me to drive through a beautiful neighbourhood. Most of Glenayr Road is covered in lovely interlock bricks which greatly adds to the charm.

2 On your way back, this stroll will make you use the Glenayr access to the park but to start this stroll, I recommend that you walk east on Millbank Avenue to admire gorgeous houses.

3 Vesta Drive, the first street you'll see on your right, is easy to miss because it looks more like a private entrance than a road.

It's a paved path offering another access to **Cedarvale Park**.

Relmar Gardens

The path leads to **Relmar Gardens**.

4 Have a peek at the prettiest "sidewalk" on your right! It runs along the front yards of lovely houses. The fact that these houses' facades face no street adds to the charm.

If you kept walking right, you'd enter **Cedarvale Park** (where you'd need to take the right fork to explore the vast park). Instead, I suggest you first get to Spadina Road to have coffee or a bite in **Forest Hill Village**.

Aroma Espresso Bar
STROLL 7
(see p. 48)

What A Bagel
STROLL 7
(see p. 48)

Pizza Banfi
STROLL 7
(see p. 48)

Take Relmar Rd. to Lonsdale Rd. and turn left to access Spadina.

Spadina Road

In case you have heard about **Hope Street Cafe** in **Forest Hill Village**, you have to know that despite the fact that it still has presence online, a new building is being built where the quaint local restaurant used to be.

5 All is not lost. An **Aroma Espresso Bar** franchise has opened nearby (383 Spadina). Its decor is modern and slick and it includes a patio. Their coffee is good! And so is the food and their attention to details. (Their cheese roll is heavenly.)

6 The little stretch across from **Aroma** is charming. I also had a peek inside **Pizza Banfi** around the corner (333 Lonsdale). It was dainty with large classic paintings and, considering the great reviews they get, I'd love to return for a fancy lunch.

7 Most of the shops along Spadina are service businesses, with a few restaurants and cafés with patios (north of Lonsdale, you'll find a **Second Cup** and a **Starbucks**).

One fun shop to visit is the independent bookstore **Type** (427 Spadina). (They also have one on Queen West near **Trinity-Bellwoods Park**.)

Suydam Park

Then, I suggest you walk north on Spadina, on its west side, to reach **Suydam Park**.

8 Walk around this park onto Strathearn Blvd. for a visual treat: the life-size bronze of two children on a bench.

Take some time to read the writings engraved in the bench. Inspiring...

Then, backtrack to **Suydam Park** and walk through it to the path leading to **Relmar Gardens**.

Take the little Relmar Road, then turn right on Lonsdale Road. It is a dead-end but you'll find a pedestrian access to Lower Village Gate (closed to the public from the evening at 9 p.m. to early morning 6 a.m.).

Lower Village Gate

9 This street is a gated loop serving a series of unique luxury condominiums. I thought it was so special and pretty that I wanted to include it in this stroll. In addition, it has its own access to the park.

Turn right on Lower Village Gate and walk around the block to a little passage on your right. You're now in **Cedarvale Park**.

10 Look left and you'll see the subway exit up the slope. Look right, this is the main trail you will follow to the vast park.

Cedarvale Park

11 Take the left fork, and you'll eventually find yourself going through the tall grass of a marsh.

You'll eventually pass under the Bathurst Viaduct.

Further west, you'll come across the bridge of Glen Cedar Road.

12 Notice the long staircase along the east side of this bridge?

It is a great workout in itself, I witnessed it put to good use by the local schools' gym teachers to torture their high school students.

13 Keep walking westbound on the path and you'll reach a vast green space with a large off-leash dog park (on your right).

I suggest you climb up the steep slope behind the dog park and turn right on Strathearn Road, to admire some more gorgeous **Forest Hill** homes.

(When I feel like starting my stroll near this section of the park, I like to park along Strathearn Road.)

14 At Glen Cedar Road, walk towards the bridge. The 1912 bridge was restored in 1989. I'm so pleased they did not destroy it. It looks amazing and kind of frozen in time.

The footbridge is wide enough for vehicles but it is now carless and offers an impressive panorama over the deep ravine.

Go down the staircase and turn left to return to your starting point.

Approximately 5 minutes past the Bathurst Bridge, you'll notice a branch on your left. Take it to get to Glenayr Road.

15 At the foot of this street, you'll love the dreamy property with spectacular landscaping. If you still have the energy, you can admire some more in the next dead-end street to your left, off Glenayr.

A small window of opportunity

The cherry on top of a Sunday (bad pun intended) at **High Park** is when you get to catch the Sakura trees in full bloom. On weekdays during the 7 to 10 days they're at their best, it feels like everyone has decided to play hooky, so you can imagine how crowded it gets on the weekends. Not to worry. Most people don't venture far from the main cherry-tree alley so there's plenty of great sights to be seen in more secluded settings all around. The other best time to stroll through **High Park** is during the fall when dark branches are contrasting against a flamboyant background.

STROLL 8

Full loop:
4.9 km (1 hr 15 min)

Shorter version:
The walk from Grenadier's parking lot down the Cherry Tree Lane by the **Grenadier Pond** and back through the gardens, is only 1 km long.

Game for more?
If you continue down Deer Pen Road from **Grenadier Restaurant**, you'll see more cherry trees along Spring Road (past the little zoo and the parking lot). It will add 1.7 km (25 min) to the stroll.

Parking & TTC
• Exit at **High Park** or **Keele Subway Stations**.
• There's a large free parking lot by **Grenadier Restaurant**. In the spring, you can also access the park from High Park Blvd and park near the zoo.

Other TIPS
• To find out when the trees are about to blossom (could be mid-April or early May!) go to **highpark-toronto.com** then look for *Cherry Blossom* under *Nature*.

The labyrinth

1 A good way to start this stroll is to walk north of the parking lot behind the **Grenadier Restaurant** to find the labyrinth on the other side of the hill. (Note that **Grenadier Restaurant** offers a wide spread of breakfast, lunch and snack options. It has a dining section, a large cafeteria with tables and a great outdoor patio.)

2 Then follow the path going south towards the road and keep going straight ahead, into the descending path. This is where you'll find the most impressive cherry trees in **High Park**.

The cherry lane

3 The lane is on a hill, which greatly adds to the appeal of the panorama before your eyes. You can see the blue water of **Grenadier Pond** at the foot of the little road. (Note that the walk down this hill is pleasant year-round.)

I've been to this section the week after the full bloom and thought it was still pretty, with a blanket of petals on the ground around the trees.

When we visited last year, a group of acrobats had brought their music and were performing amidst the flowery trees on the hill. Families were picnicking on the grass. It was a blissful afternoon.

Hillside Gardens

4 At the pond, take the first path to your left to walk up the gorgeous rockery of **Hillside Gardens**.

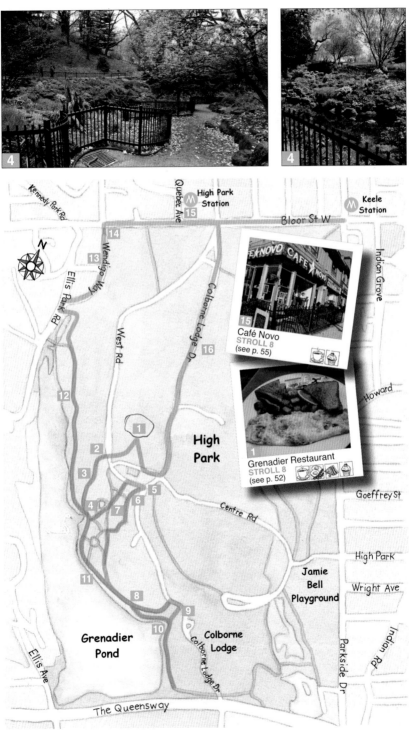

Café Novo
STROLL 8
(see p. 55)

Grenadier Restaurant
STROLL 8
(see p. 52)

It includes two small bridges, little waterfalls and a pond giving Asian vibes. The charming trail running around the rockery offers amazing views at every turn.

5 Follow the path to your right along the road by the restaurant, and walk into the trail heading down the hill, past the metal sunflowers.

6 Further down, to your left, look past the hedges to see the intriguing symmetrical garden. I never had the chance to see it in the summer but I bet it is lovely with the fountains and reflecting pool.

7 Follow the steeper fork to your left. This is where you'll get the best view of the giant maple leaf and the sinuous paths.

8 Then enter the grove and go to the pond.

Grenadier Pond

I think a stroll along **Grenadier Pond** is incomplete unless you've seen how gorgeous it is closer to The Queensway.

8 A fun way to discover it is to turn left on the large path you'll see by the pond (down the hill) and take the left fork heading up towards Colborne Lodge Drive.

9 Once you're on the drive, walk right, then right again down a staircase which leads to the pond.

10 Turn left to stroll along the banks to see the weeping willows brush the water and the ducks mingling amidst the tall grass.

11 Then, walk back along the pond, staying by the water all the way to **Wendigo Pond**.

If it's full bloom season, you'll want to walk up the Cherry Tree Lane one more time! At the top of the lane, you'll see a trail on your left which will take you straight back to the pond.

Wendigo Pond

12 As you approach **Wendigo Pond**, the grass gets taller and the wetlands more interesting.

At one point, you'll notice a parkette with a small playground on your left, turn there to reach Wendigo Way.

13 Walk northbound along this secluded street. It feels like Toronto's best kept secret. (I love to park on that fine road to enter **High Park** near **Wendigo Pond**.)

14 Time for a break, don't you think? Climb up the staircase at the end of Wendigo Way to reach Bloor Street W. and turn right.

15 Across the street awaits the cute **Café Novo**, just east of Parkview Gdns (a dead-end street with an entrance to an unstaffed platform of **High Park Subway Station**).

Colborne Lodge Dr.

16 I suggest you end the stroll by going down Colborne Lodge Drive from **High Park**'s main entrance off Bloor West.

During the cherry blossom season, you will be able to admire more marvelous trees (on the east side of the road).

MOUNT PLEASANT
CEMETERY STROLL
9

The long and winding road...

If you want to be surrounded by beauty, **Mount Pleasant Cemetery**'s picturesque stroll is for you. You won't feel like an intruder in this resting place, also a favourite amongst cyclists and joggers who use its winding paths. From the beginning (in 1876), this cemetery was designed after the 19th-century tradition of rural cemeteries and intended as a place of recreation and contemplation. **Mount Pleasant** features such a variety of trees that it qualifies as one of the biggest arboretums in Canada. No wonder the park-like cemetery is so splendid in the fall, especially on a bright sunny day.

STROLL
9

Full loop:
7.5 km (1 hr 50 min)

Shorter version:
The stroll west of the **Visitation Centre** is 5.3 km long (1 hr 20 min). The stroll east of the parking lot is 2.2 km (35 min).

Game for more?
If the 12 km of paved paths in the cemetery aren't enough, you can cross Moore Avenue, south of the **Visitation Centre**, to reach **Don Valley Evergreen Brickworks**, less than 30 min (1.8 km) further south. The **Beltline Trail** is accessible off the cemetery's entrances (at Mount Pleasant and at Yonge). You would reach Allen Rd. in 4 km.

Parking & TTC
• Exit at **St. Clair Subway Station**.
• Use the parking lot by the **Visitation Centre** as a starting point (adjacent to **25**).

Other TIPS
• The gates are open at least from 7:30 a.m. to 5:30 p.m. (they close at 8 p.m. during spring and summer).

About sections
Each section of **Mount Pleasant Cemetery** is identified with a letter or a number, nailed to a tree, relatively well in sight. Map in hand, you'll always know where you are.

Visitation Centre
A security guard confirmed to me that we can park anywhere and for as long as we want.

Nevertheless, I suggest you park at the **Visitation Centre** near section **25** to start your walk.

■1 Find the green gate of the **Forest of Remembrance** (in section **22**) to access a unique resting place where plaques on rocks commemorate those who chose cremation.

On the west side, you'll see two very elegant bronzes.

Brace yourself for what lies beyond, to your left. Sometimes marked by butterflies or pinwheels, this is the ground where babies are buried...

■2 Then, walk past the stone fountain down into the beautiful **Garden of Remembrance**. It features a vast reflecting pool, two fountains, a stream, a rockery and some gorgeous landscaping.

Sections 18 and 23
■3 At the other end of the garden, walk down the road between sections **18** and **23** and through the tunnel.

You'll emerge into the picturesque road along section **16**, on your left.

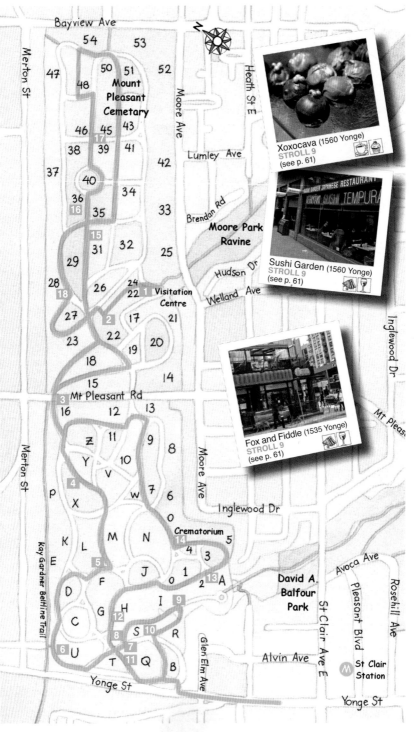

Xoxocava (1560 Yonge)
STROLL 9
(see p. 61)

Sushi Garden (1560 Yonge)
STROLL 9
(see p. 61)

Fox and Fiddle (1535 Yonge)
STROLL 9
(see p. 61)

Sections X, Y

4 Walk between **X** and **Y**. The Tree of Life on your left is one of the few modern artworks here. Look for the little girl further on your right.

5 Keep strolling between **M** and **L** and you'll get to admire the intricate work on the Massey Family Mausoleum, designed by the same architect who did **Casa Loma** and old **City Hall**).

Sections D, E

6 Go around **L** and stroll between **D** and **E** where you'll find columnar tombstones.

Further west, past the pedestrian entrance, you'll face the temple-like Thomson Mausoleum.

7 Follow the curved path running along the bucolic section **U**. Go straight towards **Q** and take the fork left of section **S**, disappearing amidst the trees.

Section S

8 Walk between the gravestones on your left for a great perspective on the sheltered mausoleums.

That's where you'll find the bronze of a golfer, undoubtedly the tribute of a loving wife.

9 At the turn of the road around **S**, you'll see on your left the original sculpture of two young firemen climbing up a ladder.

Walk up along **R** to the fork between **B** and **Q**.

10 You'll get a lovely view of the valley.

Yonge Street

Turn left on Yonge and you'll find plenty of options for a coffee or a bite within 300 metres.

There's **Second Cup** and **Starbucks**, but try **Xoxocava**, hidden in a courtyard at 1560 Yonge, for coffee and fancy chocolates. You can get good sushi at **Sushi Garden**, across from **Xoxocava**, and salads at **Freschii**, nearby on Yonge.

In the summer, how about a drink on the roof patio of **Fox and Fiddle** across the street?

Sections T and Q

11 After entering at the main entrance on your way back, turn left. Then stroll between **T** and **Q**, where the French Mausoleum faces a symmetrical garden.

Section 2

12 Walk up along **G** and **F**. (See the little boys, and the valley behind?)

13 Between **J** and **H**, take the right fork to access section **2** where a line-up of mausoleums await (including the Eaton family's).

14 Then, turn right, around the **Crematorium** and past the two beautiful women.

You'll see Alexander the Great on a horse on an imposing monument by the Mount Pleasant entrance.

Follow the road between **11** and **12** past this monument, and turn right, to go once again through the tunnel.

Sections 29 and 31

Take the right fork between **18** and **15** and turn left, past the office, towards sections **29** and **31**, where the road is lined with trees.

15 On your right, you'll see a modern statue of a man holding a bird, facing a more traditional Christ on the Cross.

16 Across, in the middle of **36**, awaits a giant religious icon, near a loyal dog by a grave.

Have a peek in the grove in circular section **40** to see granite cubes, then go eastbound.

17 Along the way, you'll notice many Chinese markers including a life-size family in section **39**.

Section 48

Turn left between sections **46** and **48** to access a section featuring low walls which form a cross; look it up on Google Satellite! (Look for lanterns around these walls.)

Turn right around **50**, into the pretty path between **50** and **51**. Keep going, then turn right around section **35**.

Section 27

18 Walk between **27** and **28**, past the turquoise semi-circle in **28**, for a great view and a look at a stone... tire.

Go with the flow!

There's something utterly relaxing about strolling by a river and **Humber River** offers just the right setting. Long trails allow us to walk on both banks of the river. The river is wide enough to sparkle under the sun, and sinuous enough to offer a different view at every turn. The panoramas are unique. Park benches invite you to stop and listen to the stream. **Old Mill Bridge** and **Inn** add architectural interest. Signs in **Étienne Brûlé Park** give a bit of history of the first French to have settled in Ontario. **Ma Maison** on Dundas West proves it was a good thing!... With a line-up of the best French pastries.

Full loop:
6.7 km (1 hr 40 min)

Shorter version:
From **Étienne Brûlé Park**'s parking lot to Dundas and back, it's 4.5 km (1 hr 10 min).

Game for more?
At the end of **Étienne Brûlé Park** (following the trail under the Dundas Bridge) you'll enter **Lambton Park**, then **James Gardens** further north (thanks to a pedestrian bridge). To get to **James Gardens** and back will add 3.4 km (50 min) to the stroll.

Parking & TTC
• Exit at **Old Mill Subway Station** and walk north.
• There's free parking in **Étienne Brûlé Park**.

Other TIPS
• You can enjoy the **Old Mill Inn**'s decor and good food for breakfast from 7:30 a.m. to 10:30 a.m. (M-Sat.), weekdays for lunch 12 noon to 2:30 p.m., daily afternoon tea and Sunday brunch. Their cosy **Home Smith Bar** is open for drinks from at least 3 p.m.

Old Mill Bridge

1 The arched stone **Old Mill Bridge** going over the **Humber River** dates back to 1916. You can access the free parking lot of **Étienne Brûlé Park** on its east side.

I suggest you first walk along the west bank of the river, for a more dramatic effect. So you need to walk over the bridge into Old Mill Road.

2 You will pass by the **Old Mill Inn**, standing like a collection of charming old English cottages.

Then keep your right to enter Home Smith Park Road.

Home Smith Park

3 The quiet road runs along a stone wall nicely covered with ivy and follows the sinuous bed of **Humber River** into **Home Smith Park**.

4 You'll find benches at different turns to admire the river.

Six low dams, spread along the course of the stream between Old Mill Road and Dundas Street, control its flow, hence the lovely sound of cascades you'll hear as you walk.

Weeping willows occasionally brush the water. And there's enough trees around to offer a splendid walk during the fall.

5 Feeling a bit adventurous? Past the little parking lot to your right (closer to Dundas Street West), you'll see a dirt trail going down. Follow it to reach the viaduct (beware, it becomes steep and possibly slippery).

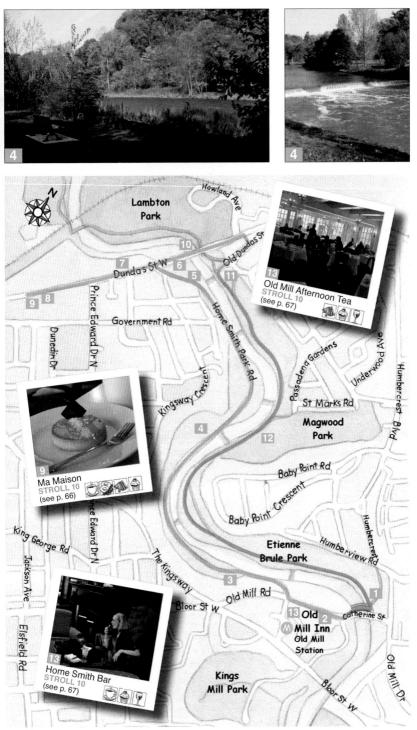

Lambton
Park

Old Mill Afternoon Tea
STROLL 10
(see p. 67)

Ma Maison
STROLL 10
(see p. 66)

Home Smith Bar
STROLL 10
(see p. 67)

Howland Ave

Old Dundas St

Dundas St W

Government Rd

Prince Edward Dr N

Dunedin Dr

Home Smith Park Rd

Kingsway Crescent

Passadena Gardens

Underwood Ave

Humbercrest Blvd

St Marks Rd

Magwood
Park

Baby Point Rd

Baby Point Crescent

King George Rd

Prince Edward Dr N

The Kingsway

Jackson Ave

Elsfield Rd

Etienne
Brule Park

Humberview Rd

Humbercrest

Old Mill Rd

Bloor St W

Old Mill Inn
Old Mill
Station

Catherine St

Kings
Mill Park

Bloor St W

Old Mill Dr

6 At the foot of the viaduct, you'll see interesting graffiti and looking across the river, you'll get a unique perspective of the bridge's arches.

Return to Home Smith Park Road and turn right to get to Dundas Street West.

Dundas Street West

Dundas Street in this part of town does not have much to recommend itself but just enough to convince me to suggest you turn left.

7 You'll walk past retro looking **Swirls Cupcakes** at 4158 Dundas W., very well worth a take-out on your way back, but we're aiming for **Ma Maison** (4243 Dundas W., .6 km from the bridge).

8 It will be on your left, past the bike mural and **Gibson's Cleaners** topped with a life-size moose (a survivor of the invasion of the fiberglass moose art event in Toronto in 2000).

9 The authentic pâtisserie/boulangerie/traiteur, run by a Toulouse-born chef, seems out of its element in the concrete world of Etobicoke but everything is "ze reel ting" in this cute French café.

Note that it is closed on Sundays and Mondays. On both days, you can go to **Java Joe's**, next to **Mastermind Toys** across the street.

The European invasion doesn't stop here. You will also find **Daniel Le Chocolat Belge** (4242 Dundas W.) open every day and offering a wide variety of Belgian chocolates with fillings.

10 After all these treats, you can now "roll" back eastbound on Dundas Street and over the bridge, for a spectacular view of **Humber River**.

At Howland, past the bridge, you'll see a paved path on your right. Take it to Old Dundas Street and turn right (you'll walk by **Lambton House**).

11 At the foot of the dead-end street, you'll see an opening straight ahead, with steps going down to the river.

Follow the trail going left along the river. (The paved path on your right leads to **Lambton Park**.)

Magwood and Étienne Brûlé Parks

12 The pedestrian path will run parallel to a bike trail once you reach a clearing. Further east, trees get more mature in the groves of **Magwood Park**, which gives a nice country feel to the path.

You'll eventually reach **Étienne Brûlé Park** (named after the first French to explore Ontario beyond the St. Lawrence River).

Old Mill Inn

If you've chosen not to go to **Ma Maison**, you might consider stopping at the **Old Mill Inn**. They serve breakfast, lunch and dinner in their main dining room.

13 They offer a fancy afternoon tea daily in a special room. In the summer, there's also the outdoor **Old Mill Tea Garden**.

Past 3 p.m., you can have a bite and a drink in **Home Smith Bar**'s cozy chairs.

ROSEDALE VALLEY
FALL COLOURS STROLL
11

Where an urban stroll gets scenic!

The first time I drove into Rosedale Valley Road, off Yonge Street, I just couldn't believe the contrast between the frenzy of Yonge and the sheltered country feeling of this road nestled at the bottom of a ravine. It took me a while to figure out the best way to access it on foot but here it is: my favourite way to enjoy one of Toronto's best hidden gems. Actually, make that two! This walk includes another of Toronto's best kept secrets: **Wellesley Park** in Cabbagetown. Rosedale Valley Road is splendid during the fall colours but it will offer a great stroll at any time of the year.

STROLL
11

Full loop:
6.6 km (1 hr 40 min)

Shorter version:
The pedestrian bridge is right in the middle of the long stroll. You can walk from any end to the little bridge and back in 3.3 km (50 min).

Game for more?
From **Wellesley Park**, you can explore beautiful **Cabbagetown**. Last time I did this stroll, we walked west to Parliament and then south and had a wonderful lunch at **House on Parliament** (at 454 Parliament), 1 km away from the park.

Parking & TTC
• Exit at **Bloor Subway Station** (**Sherbourne Station** is only good if the staircase at Mount Pleasant is open).
• I usually find free parking on Sumach St. in **Cabbagetown**.

Other TIPS
• If the Main Sanctuary is closed when you visit **St. Paul's Bloor Street Church**, ask to take a peek. They might let you in if they're not too busy.

Wellesley Park

I prefer starting this stroll from **Cabbagetown**. I can always find street parking space north of **Riverdale Farm**. (Try parking on Sumach Street, by **Wellesley Park**.)

1 I suggest you take a little peek around Sumach and Wellesley Streets to enjoy one of Toronto's loveliest neighbourhoods.

2 Then, walk into sheltered **Wellesley Park** at the foot of Amelia Street. You'll see a line-up of houses. Notice anything different? They're not fronting a street like any other houses; their front yards directly border the park.

3 On the northeast corner of the park, a hidden wooden staircase will lead you to Rosedale Valley Road.

Rosedale Valley Rd.

4 A sidewalk runs along the south side of Rosedale Valley Road, all the way up to Park Road, 2 kms further west.

Rosedale Valley Road is long and winding with hardly any pedestrians. But it's in fact a busy boulevard masquerading as a country road. I dared crossing it to examine a curious altar on a tree on its north side (with flowers and photo but no explanation). It took me forever to have enough time between cars.

The road is towered over by tall trees, which makes for a spectacular panorama in the fall. At other times, it is still unique enough to be visited for a great walk.

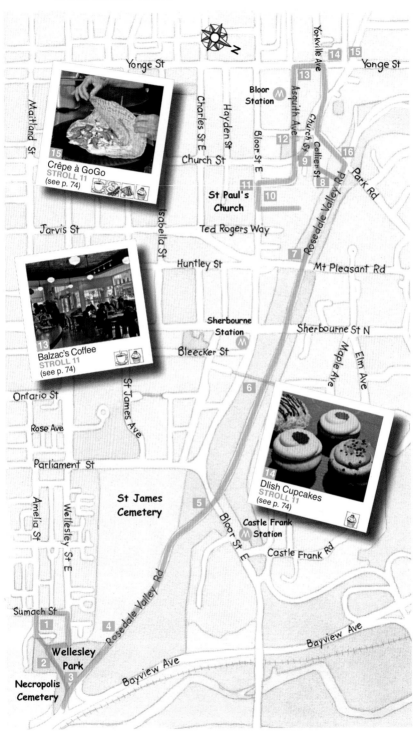

15
Crêpe à GoGo
STROLL 11
(see p. 74)

13
Balzac's Coffee
STROLL 11
(see p. 74)

14
Dlish Cupcakes
STROLL 11
(see p. 74)

Yonge St
Yonge St
Maitland St
Charles St E
Hayden St
Bloor Station
Asquith Ave
Yorkville Ave
14 **15**
Yonge St
13
Bloor St E
Church St
Church St E
Collier St
12
16
9
8
Park Rd
Church St
11 **10**
St Paul's Church
Jarvis St
Isabella St
Ted Rogers Way
Huntley St
Mt Pleasant Rd
7
Rosedale Valley Rd
Sherbourne Station
Sherbourne St N
Bleecker St
Maple Ave
Elm Ave
Ontario St
St James Ave
6
Rose Ave
Parliament St
St James Cemetery
14
Amelia St
Wellesley St E
5
Bloor St E
Castle Frank Station
Castle Frank Rd
Sumach St
1
4
Rosedale Valley Rd
Bayview Ave
2
Wellesley Park
Bayview Ave
3
Necropolis Cemetery

On your left, you'll see an old section of **St. James Cemetery** (which I think would fit the bill in a vampire movie).

5 The Bloor overpass (the first bridge you'll see) is impressive with its strong black steel structure. It is followed by a bridge supporting the subway line.

6 Further west, you'll pass under a pedestrian bridge which links St. James Town to Rosedale.

Next is the Sherbourne overpass. I climbed up the unofficial steep trail reaching Bloor at Sherbourne to see how it went. Not the prettiest sight, with all the garbage laying around, but it brought out the Davy Crockett in me.

7 Then you'll reach the Mount Pleasant viaduct. If you get closer to the foot of the bridge, you'll see a staircase on the right side which leads to Bloor Street. (Note that it was under construction at the time of print.)

If you climb up these stairs, you'll be able to admire two pretty landscape murals along Mount Pleasant down below (on the northwest and southeast sides of Bloor Street).

8 Past an indoor parking lot you'll see a clearing. Look carefully and you'll notice a few steps in the grass. They will take you to Collier Street.

Collier Street

9 Collier is a lovely dead-end street set with benches and looking into the courtyard of the **Manulife** building.

Walk west on Collier and take the first lane to your left.

Turn left on Church Street and you'll reach cute **Milner Parkette**. Take Asquith Avenue to your left just around the corner. The elbow street becomes St. Paul's Square.

St. Paul's Square

10 Depending on the time of the day and the week, you can access the manicured grounds of **Manulife's Head Office** from two entrances off St. Paul's Square.

Otherwise, just walk around and enter the courtyard from Bloor Street. You'll pass by one of my favourite sculptures in Toronto: *Community* by Kirk Newman. (Take a minute to enjoy the humour in the lively crowd where playing kids mingle with busy business men attached to their cell phones.)

11 Across the street is **St. Paul's Bloor Street Church**, one of Toronto's finest examples of integration of old and new architecture. Love it!

In 2002, the Anglican community launched elegant renovations to link the oldest church, built in 1858, to the newer church, built in 1913 (it is the work of Lennox, the same architect who did old City Hall and Casa Loma).

The Main Sanctuary is splendid but normally open only on Sundays.

The Atrium between the two churches is generally open and it allows you to peek into the courtyard.

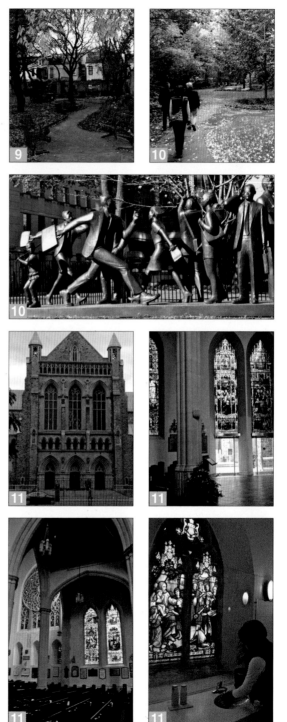

You will be able to admire the outdoor court-yard from the bay windows in the foyer and the small chapel. Even the bath-rooms are worth a visit! They include gorgeous stain glass windows.

Asquith Park

12 Back on St. Paul's Square, return to Asquith Ave. and cross Church St. to get to the little **Asquith Green Park**, fea-turing interesting public art.

Yonge Street

13 Further west is Yonge. Turn right and you'll find the latest **Balzac's Coffee** inside the **Toronto Reference Library** (with a soothing fountain).

14 Across the street, you'll find a lovely little stretch along Yorkville Ave-nue. It includes **Dlish Cup-cakes** next to **Cookbook Store** (850 Yonge), and a designer shop featuring the avant-garde fashion of **Ula Zukowska** (5 Yorkville Avenue).

15 Across the street is **Crêpes à GoGo** (18 Yorkville), serving scrump-tious thin French crêpes (and a great place to prac-tise your French).

I suggest you grab one to go and walk to nearby **Town Hall Square**, graced with a huge tree sculpture and giant pots.

Park Road

16 To return to Rosedale Valley Road, take Church Street and follow Collier to get to Park Road, where you'll turn left to the ravine road.

THE BEACH
SOOTHING STROLL

A break from urban life

Stressed out by the compulsive busyness of your life? This waterfront stroll will do the trick! There's nothing more soothing than the noise of waves brushing the shore and nothing so relaxing as the sight of sparkling water. Letting your eyes scan the endless horizon is like meditation. All of this creates the perfect conditions for the best conversations with your friends. Rule of thumb, the further east you'll walk along **The Beach**'s boardwalk, the farther you'll get away from the crowd. This walk also includes a few dips into Queen Street to indulge with French pastries or yummy salty muffins. Also very soothing...

STROLL
12

Full loop:
8 km (2 hrs)

Shorter version:
The stroll segment east of **Kew Gardens** is 3.6 km long (55 min).

Game for more?
Upper Beach Steep Hill Stroll (Stroll 24, p. 147) is just a few minutes north of this stroll. (Take Glen Manor Drive off the boardwalk.)

Parking & TTC
• The streetcar **#501** runs along Queen E.
• I can usually find free street parking on the streets in the new development just east of **Woodbine Park**, south of Queen Street.
• The further east you go, past **Kew Gardens**, the easier it is to find free parking spots on the streets south of Queen Street.

Other TIPS
• The **Fox Theatre** is an independent movie theatre located at 2236 Queen Street East (between Willow and Beech Avenues). Visit **foxtheatre.ca** for their listings. They often do a 6:45 p.m. presentation.

Queen East

1 I recommend you start this stroll hungry so you can enjoy a café au lait and a croissant at French **Zane Patisserie** (1852 Queen E.). If you end the stroll in this part of town, consider taking out some of their scrumptious pastries!

You can easily find free parking spots south of Queen Street, on the streets east of **Woodbine Park**. Boardwalk Drive is the closest to the bakery.

Back alley walk

2 Walk south on Boardwalk Drive and turn into the lane on your left to access the cheerful back alley of this new development, on your right.

3 At the foot of Joseph Duggan Road, you'll see a pedestrian access to Lake Shore Boulevard. You can cross at the light to reach the boardwalk.

Boardwalk stroll

4 **The Beach**'s boardwalk starts at the eastern end of **Woodbine Beach** and goes up to Silver Birch, 3 kms further east.

You never know what you'll come across when strolling along this boardwalk. You could see some rogue art in the form of rock sculptures defying gravity or a pebble labyrinth lined in the sand.

Once, in one outing, I saw a man gracefully manoeuvring a stunt kite and a girl flying her Tinker Bell kite. Two happy couples in wedding clothes posed for their photographer.

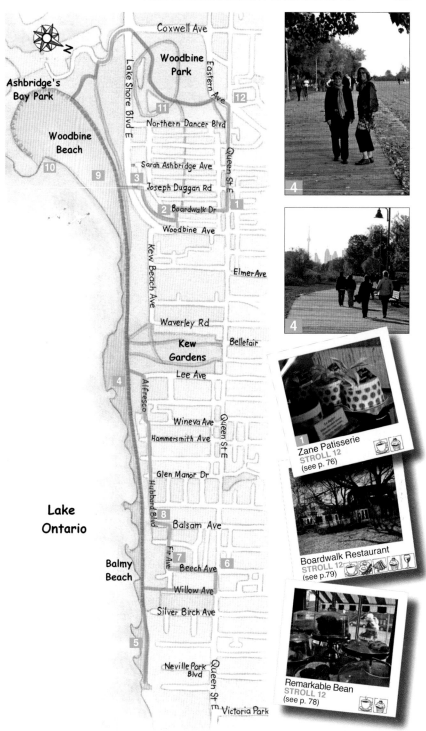

Coxwell Ave

Woodbine Park

Eastern Ave

Ashbridge's Bay Park

Lake Shore Blvd E

Woodbine Beach

Northern Dancer Blvd

Sarah Ashbridge Ave

Joseph Duggan Rd

Boardwalk Dr

Woodbine Ave

Kew Beach Ave

Elmer Ave

Waverley Rd

Kew Gardens

Bellefair

Lee Ave

Queen St E

Alfresco

Wineva Ave

Hammersmith Ave

Glen Manor Dr

Hubbard Blvd

Lake Ontario

Balsam Ave

Fir Ave

Beech Ave

Balmy Beach

Willow Ave

Silver Birch Ave

Neville Park Blvd

Queen St E

Victoria Park

Queen St E

Zane Patisserie
STROLL 12
(see p.76)

Boardwalk Restaurant
STROLL 12
(see p.79)

Remarkable Bean
STROLL 12
(see p.78)

A family of musicians played before passersby.

Expect Christmas lights on the trees in the winter near Balsam Avenue.

Beach houses

5 The boardwalk ends past the **Balmy Beach Club** but you can still walk on the sand, admiring dreamy beach houses along the way. (Some of them have infinity pools!)

This segment of the beach is much more secluded.

Queen East again

If you've not stopped at **Zane**, you might be ready for salty muffins at **Remarkable Bean** (2242 Queen E.). To get there, walk back west and go north on Willow Avenue (the second street you can access from the boardwalk). Then turn left on Queen East.

6 If the weather is warm, you may consider a visit to **Ed's Real Scoop** for some serious ice cream or gelato (2224 Queen E.).

Fir Avenue

7 Take Beech Avenue towards the lake and turn right into Fir Avenue at **Balmy Beach Park**. (That's an impressive balcony on the house at the corner of Fir and Beech, isn't it?)

Strolling down the beachfront streets will give you a glimpse of the lifestyle of The Beach's residents.

8 At Balsam Ave., take the turn into Hubbard.

Further west, keep your left to continue into Alfresco Lawn and return to the boardwalk.

Woodbine Beach

9 The beach is at its widest at **Woodbine Beach**. It is where most people hang out. That's where you'll see volleyball nets. It's also where you can see fireworks on Canada Day.

The **Boardwalk Restaurant** (across from **Woodbine Park**) is the only one by the beach, if you don't consider the three snack bars along the boardwalk (at the outdoor pool of **Donald D. Summerville**, at the foot of **Kew Gardens**, and near **Balmy Beach**).

At the time of print, the restaurant was still undergoing the construction of a major extension. From the look of it, it will increase the size of the patio (one great reason to stop there for a bite).

10 My favourite part of **Woodbine Beach** is the bay closer to the large boulders at the entrance of **Ashbridge's Bay Park**. We've added many picnics there with friends while waiting for the sun to set.

Woodbine Park

11 Follow the paved path to Lake Shore Blvd., to reach **Woodbine Park** (where you'll want to walk through the tall grass to see the fountain in the large pond around the hill on your right).

12 You could end the stroll with a drink on **Murphy's Law Irish Pub**'s rooftop (1702 Queen E.).

The "not so Greek" Danforth

If you don't live in the area, to you Danforth Avenue is probably all about Greek restaurants and the **Taste of the Danforth** event. But to the locals, it's a busy street where they can find anything they need (thanks to a line-up of specialty stores and food shops) before returning to the tranquil oasis of their home through a grid of quiet back lanes and secluded pedestrian paths. Add to this the gorgeous **Withrow Park**, beautiful houses and out-of-the-way little cafés, and you get the perfect stroll to work up your appetite before entering one of over thirty restaurants and pubs on Danforth.

STROLL
13

Full loop:
5.9 km (1 hr 30 min)

Shorter version:
If you skip the park section south of Danforth, the stroll will be 3.5 km long (55 min). If you choose instead not to go further west than **The Big Carrot**, the walk drops to 3 km (45 min).

Game for more?
Walk south of Danforth on Broadview Avenue and you'll reach **Riverdale Park East** in a few minutes. A footbridge running over the Don Valley Parkway will lead you to **Cabbagetown**.

Parking & TTC
• Exit at **Chester** or **Broadview Subway Stations**.
• I usually find free street parking south of **Withrow Park**.

Other TIPS
• **The Danforth Music Hall** (147 Danforth) is a dynamic venue of over 1,000 seats featuring all kinds of shows (from musicals, to Led Zeppelin tribute to fundraisers). For their programming, see **thedanforth.com**.

Riverdale Avenue

South of **Withrow Park**, further from busy Danforth Avenue, it's easier to find free street parking. But my main reason for wanting to start the stroll at this end is out-of-the-way **Riverdale Perk Café** (633 Logan at Withrow Avenue).

1 The cute café blends perfectly with the surrounding houses. It serves great coffee and delectable treats and light meals.

Just east of Logan are a set of lanes going up from Simpson Avenue to **Withrow Park**, which get particularly pretty from Riverdale Avenue (off the map) up to the park.

2 As you walk up the lane north of Riverdale Avenue, you get the feeling of being in the narrow street of a small village. Many trees lean from the private backyards over the alley and instead of a boring line-up of garages, we see 3-storey houses in the perspective.

3 Thanks to the plateaus formed by the streets crossing the lanes north and south of Withrow, passersby seem to disappear as they walk up or down the hilly alleyways.

Withrow Park

4 The lane north of Bain Avenue leads to **Withrow Park**'s long staircase.

From up there, you get a nice view of the large properties on Logan Avenue across from the park.

Further north on the paved path, you'll oversee a big off-leash dog park by a grove of mature trees.

Nealon Ave

Fulton Ave

Chester Hill Rd

Thorncliffe Ave

Browning Ave

14

Cambridge Ave

13

Broadview Ave

12

Pretoria Ave

Playter Cr

Playter Blvd

11

Jackman Ave

Don Valley Pkwy

Riverdale Perk Café
STROLL 13
(see p. 82)
1

Chester Ave

Arundel Ave

Logan Ave

Carlaw Ave

Gough Ave

9

10

Chester
Station

16

Broadview
Station

Danforth Ave

17   **6**   **8**   **7**

15

18

Dearbourne Ave

Bowden St

Hampton Ave

Gamock Ave

Walfrey Ave

Mc Connell Ave

Fenwick Ave

Logan Ave

Withrow
Park

Carlaw Ave

Broadview Espresso
STROLL 13
(see p. 85)
12

Allen's
STROLL 13
(see p. 86)

5

4

Bain Ave

Riverdale
Park West

Don Valley Pkwy

Broadview Ave

1

Withrow Ave

3

2

5 Walk across the park to have a closer look at the houses on Carlaw Avenue, then stroll towards the playground along McConnell Avenue on the north side of **Withrow Park**.

Take Fenwick Avenue northbound to Danforth Avenue and turn right. Here's your chance to visit one of Danforth's iconic places (to women, anyway): **Sophie's Lingerie**, the specialists in bra fitting at 527 Danforth. (Many of us are clueless in this department!)

A bit further east is **Nharo!**, a unique shop selling fair-trade African art.

6 Across the street is my favourite cluster of shops. It includes the stylish housewares store **iQ living** (542 Danforth) right next to the garden lifestyle **Moss** and quaint used book and music shop **Re: Reading**.

That's where you'll find **Pizzeria Libretto** (550 Danforth), featuring the best urban sleek decor on the street and famous for their unique pizza baked in 90 seconds in a 900 degree wood-burning oven. Open for lunch and dinner. Yum!

7 **Holy Name Parish**, the church you can see east of **Starbucks** gives much character to the neighbourhood.

On your way there, there's **Maxi** (575 Danforth, on the south side). This is one of Toronto's best places east of the Don Valley to admire dreamy fashion. It sits next to **Treasure Island Toys**, an excellent toy store.

8 Turn north on Gough Avenue (at the church) to get to the parkettes. On your left, you'll notice the exotic facade of the small **Greek Orthodox Church of St. Irene Chrysovalantou**. (It used to be a car shop!)

Through parkettes

9 Past the tiny Greek church, on your left, you'll find **Carlaw Avenue Parkette**, the first of four parkettes located just north of Danforth Avenue.

The paved path runs through cute little parks and small municipal parking lots up to **Chester Subway Station**, allowing locals to avoid the busy main street.

Keep walking along the paved path on the north side of the station. It leads to Jackman Avenue.

10 Have a peek into the lane to your right.

11 Follow Hurndale Ave., west of Jackman and turn right on Player Blvd. It will take you to Player Crescent. Do the full loop to see the impressive properties in this part of **The Danforth**!

Pretoria Avenue

12 Stay on your left to reach Pretoria, past Ellerbeck Street. **Broadview Espresso** (817 Broadview) serves great coffee at the corner of Pretoria and Broadview.

13 Straight across Broadview, turn right on Cambridge Avenue. (I like the line-up of tiny houses north of Eastmount Avenue.) Then turn left on Thorncliffe Avenue.

14 You deserve a fun surprise for having come this far and it awaits at Chester Hill Road. On your left is a belvedere overlooking the Don Valley and **Evergreen Brick Works** on your right. On a clear day, you can admire the **CN Tower** above the cityscape to your left.

You can also see a large compass slowly fading on the asphalt of the roundabout. Victor Fraser, an original local street artist, painted it a few years ago.

Danforth Avenue

Back to Pretoria, turn right on Broadview.

Not to be missed south of Danforth for potential vintage finds are **Tabula Rasa** (745 Broadview), and **Der Dietemann**.

In summertime, **Allen's** patio is fantastic (143 Danforth) and so is **Globe Bistro**'s chic roof patio (124).

15 We loved **Factory Girl**'s room in the back (193).

16 Between Playter and Logan, you'll find over twelve great fashion stores with original selection (including **Trove** at 393). The **Carrot Common** (in the middle, at 348 Danforth) hosts the area's landmark **Big Carrot** and **Book City**.

17 Let's not forget we are in **Greektown**. Expect fifteen Greek restaurants between Chester and Carlaw.

18 Consider a foamy latte at **Crema** (508) while people watching, and a take-out of honey balls at **Athens Pastries** across the street, before heading south on Logan.

EDWARDS GARDENS
MANSIONS STROLL

It doesn't cost to have a look

In the 50s, businessman Rupert Edwards sold his estate garden to the City, which eventually turned it into the beautiful **Edwards Gardens** and opened it to the public. When you exit the gardens off the western entrance, you walk into the world of another kind of estates: the private two-acre lots of the very wealthy living in **The Bridle Path**. Think multi-million-dollar mansions, spectacular iron gates, manicured lawns and serious landscaping. You can't "blend in" when strolling in this secluded part of town but it's the kind of stroll sure to initiate lively conversations with your friends.

Full loop:
4.8 km (1 hr 15 min)

Shorter version:
To cut the stroll down to 2.6 km (40 min), don't do the section north of Lawrence and return to **Edwards Gardens**. Walk back to the bridge, cross over the pond and turn right. Then climb the first staircase to your left to get back to the parking lot.

Game for more?
Wilket Creek Park is accessible from the path which runs southbound on the east part of **Edwards Gardens**. The wilderness 1.5 km trail will lead you to **Serena Gundy Park**.

Parking & TTC
• The bus line **#54** runs along Lawrence Avenue East.
• Parking is free at **Edwards Gardens**.

Other TIPS
• Consult **torontobotanicalgarden.ca/events** for a list of events and workshops organized by the **Toronto Botanical Garden**.

Edwards Gardens

The entrance to **Edwards Gardens** is located on Lawrence Avenue East, just east of Leslie Street.

Most people confuse **Toronto Botanical Garden (TBG)** with **Edwards Gardens** but they're actually two separate entities.

Edwards Gardens is a public place belonging to the City of Toronto while **TBG** is a private not-for-profit volunteer-based organization dedicated to gardening. (The building itself is usually open 9 a.m. to 5 p.m. on weekdays and 12 noon to 5 p.m. on weekends.)

1 Before heading towards the gardens, make sure to explore the original entry garden filled with interesting textures and adorned by a whimsical sculpture by Ron Baird.

2 Then visit the Westview Terrace, the courtyard on the west side of **TBG** where you'll find a lovely water canal (and from which you'll be able to observe a green roof if you're looking south).

3 The Knot Garden is noticeable with its swirls of precisely shaped hedges.

4 You'll walk by the **Garden Café** on your way down the valley in the western part of the park. I'm always impressed by the size of the willow tree in the middle of this valley.

5 Follow the long loop and it will take you to one of the prettiest viewpoints in **Edwards Gardens**, with a rockery, a few bridges, flowers and trails.

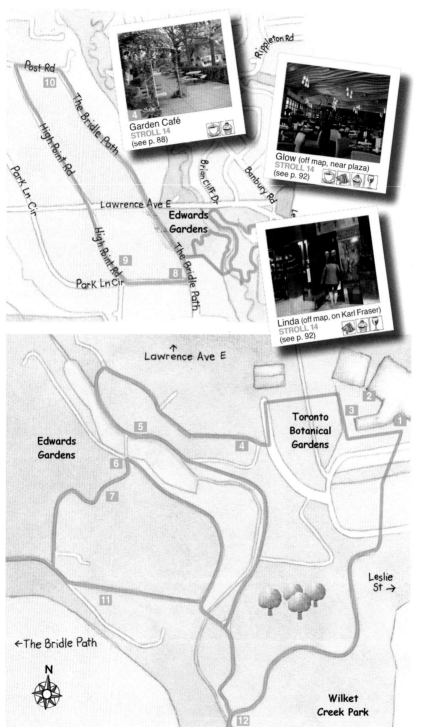

Garden Café
STROLL 14
(see p. 88)

Glow (off map, near plaza)
STROLL 14
(see p. 92)

Linda (off map, on Karl Fraser)
STROLL 14
(see p. 92)

Lawrence Ave E

Edwards
Gardens

Toronto
Botanical
Gardens

Leslie
St →

←The Bridle Path

N

Wilket
Creek Park

Don't cross the first bridge. Keep going eastbound to enjoy the wonderful rockery on your left, with the sinuous stream on your right.

Take the second bridge to your right and walk back northbound on the west bank to return to the wooden bridge you first saw.

6 You'll notice a staircase on your left. Take it to reach the children's Teaching Garden.

7 This section of **Edwards Gardens** is a beautiful little easy-to-miss oasis. It is set near the towering white pine trees and the red-roofed garden house. (It includes a sandpit, dinosaur footprints and a giant monarch butterfly.)

Further up the trail, you'll come across a fork. Turn right to walk towards the street to get to the mansions part of this stroll.

Park Lane Circle

The western entrance to **Edwards Gardens** is located on The Bridle Path. We often hear people calling it the "Bridal Path" but the name refers to the bridle of a horse. (The original owners were horse-owners and the upscale neighbourhood was initially planned to include equestrian paths.)

8 Turn left on The Bridle Path and walk right, around the corner onto Park Lane Circle.

Aren't the life-size sculptures of a horse and grazing lamb on the manicured lawn the perfect intro to this tour?

Further west, to your left, you'll be able to peek at a Poseidon statue in the entrance of a gigantic mansion.

High Point Road

9 Turn right on High Point Road. From then on, you'll only get glimpses of the multi-million dollar residences on the estates but you'll be able to admire gorgeous iron gates.

Apparently, The Bridle Path is the part of Toronto with the most properties worth $10 M and over. I read that the estate at 9 High Point Road was listed at $27 M in 2011 and includes indoor tennis courts and pool, bowling alley and movie theatre.

The host of HGTV's *Mansions* listed his estate at 37 High Point Road for $23 M. Its master bedroom is over 3 000 sq. ft (with a bar) and the mansion includes a 4,500 sq. ft. indoor pool!

As we were walking northbound on this road, the only people we saw were a nanny with a little boy driving an electric car, a mailman driving from one estate to the next to drop the mail, and a delivery man waiting at a gate.

He waited and waited. No one answered during the ten minutes we could see him as we strolled by.

The man was delivering a Ferrari!

Now THIS puts things into perspective. I'm home when I know they're delivering a $1,000 washing machine to me!

The Bridle Path

Once you reach Post Road, I suggest you turn right to get to The Bridle Path. (Were you to turn left, then left again, you'd reach Park Lane Circle. This is the street the likes of Prince, Gordon Lightfoot and Conrad Black have called home but most of the properties are hidden behind a wall of trees.)

 You'll see plenty of gorgeous gates along The Bridle Path as you walk back to the Gardens.

Back to the Gardens

11 Take the right fork by the Teaching Garden to get down to the creek, then turn right.

12 Walk over the bridge you'll see past the sign for **Wilket Creek Park** and into the woods to your left, to have a closer look at the creek. (In the fall on a sunny day, it is at its best.)

Then I suggest you return to the parking lot by taking the path going up to your right (located south of the maintenance house).

Shops at Don Mills

The **Garden Café** is open seasonally (May-October, from 10 a.m. to 4 p.m.).

But after such a stroll amongst the wealthy, I recommend you drive to **Shops at Don Mills** (not on map, 1.2 km eastbound on Lawrence East) to get a fancy lunch or treat.

We enjoyed the food and decor at **Glow** (they have a great patio) but there are many more options. Beautiful **Linda Modern Thai** is next on my list!

HARBORD VILLAGE
DOLCE VITA STROLL
15

A good stroll for property envy!

This stroll takes you through charming residential pockets sandwiched between Harbord and College, two vibrant streets offering plenty of unique restaurants and original shops. Most of the properties are set on small lots, adorned with quaint front porches and all kinds of lovely architectural detail which you'll see if you think to look up. The trees often form an arch of leaves over the sidewalks. Here and there, there's elaborate street art to be admired if you peek into the lanes. The walk also includes great cafés, good places for cocktails, plenty of patios, a large park and a sneak into **Little Italy**.

STROLL
15

Full loop:
7 km (1 hr 45 min)

Shorter version:
If you leave out the park section and the walk west of Grace, it will be a 5 km stroll (1 hr 15 min).

Game for more?
The **Kensington Market** is south of College Street, down Augusta Avenue, just east of Brunswick Avenue.

Parking & TTC
• The streetcar **#506** runs along College Street.
• I usually find free parking spaces along Grace Street.

Other TIPS
• **The Royal** movie theatre (at 608 College Street, east of Grace) is a second-run independent cinema. They usually feature a matinee on Sundays. See their listing on **theroyal.to**.
• **Harbord Village** is between Bloor and College (and Bathurst and Spadina). **Little Italy** is set between Ossington and Bathurst (from Dundas to a bit south of Harbord).

Bickford Park

1 Try to find street parking along Grace, south of Harbord and get a warm-up by strolling around **Bickford Park** (especially lovely during the fall).

There used to be a cool café, **Linuxcaffe**, at the corner of Harbord and Grace but it has closed. (My guess is it will be replaced by another café.)

2 Go west on Harbord and turn right onto the path going around the park.

3 Walk back to Harbord along Grace, then left on Harbord Street. If **Rebecca Gallery** is open (317 Grace), you might want to drop in to admire the art in the airy space.

4 Further east on Harbord, I usually grab a coffee at **Sam James Coffee Bar**. (Check funky **Harbord Coinwash** across the street.)

Then turn right on Manning to access lovely Ulster Street.

Ulster Street

One has to be on foot to really enjoy Ulster (its one-ways change direction at every block between Manning Ave. and Major St.).

I love the view we get at every corner and into every lane.

5 I recommend you take a tour around one of the prettiest blocks in the neighbourhood by going south on Palmerston Boulevard, east on College Street.

6 Then go north on Markham Street.

Crawford St
Montrose Ave
Crawford St
Montrose Ave
Beatrice St
Harbord St
2 **Bickford Park**
23
22
24 **Grace St** **1** **Grace St**
College St
21 **3** **Jersey Ave**
20 **Clinton St**
4
22 Fish Store & Sandwiches
STROLL 15
(see p. 98)
Manning Ave
19
Euclid Ave
Ulster St
17 No One Writes to the Colonel
STROLL 15
(see p. 98)
18 Palmerston Blvd
5
Markham St
6
17
Bathurst St
10 DT Bistro
STROLL 15
(see p. 96)
16
15 Lippincott St
Lennox St
12 Croft St
13
14 Borden St **7**
8
College St
Ulster St
Brunswick Ave **9**
Sussex Ave
11
Major St
10
Robert St
Kosower Ln
Harbord St
Spadia Crescent
Sussex Mews

And return to finish your stroll on Ulster, then turn left on Borden St. to Harbord.

Harbord Street

7 **Chabichou**, a fine cheese and gourmet food shop with tables, stands proud at the corner of Borden and Harbord.

8 **The Boulevard Café**, the Peruvian eatery at 161 Harbord is so appealing with its patio and exotic mural. It's high on my list of places to try for an afternoon drink.

I'm also a big fan of the rooftop patio of French **Tati Bistro** (124 Harbord). Not open for lunch but they do weekend brunches.

9 When I learned that DT stands for Dessert Trends in **DT Bistro**, I had to try the place! The desserts are indeed spectacular, the rest of the menu delicious and the decor fun and feminine (154 Harbord, open from at least 11 a.m. Wednesday to Sunday).

Next is **Harbord House**, a casual place with great food, also open for lunch. **Harbord Bakery** (115 Harbord) has been an institution in this neighbourhood since 1945.

There's also plenty of food for thought to be found in niche bookstores: **Parentbooks** (all about parenting at 201 Harbord), **Caversham** (all about mental health at 98 Harbord), **Wonderworks** offering body/mind/wellness books (79A Harbord) and **Bakka Phoenix Books** selling science fiction and fantasy books (84 Harbord).

The **Toronto Women's Bookstore** unfortunately closed in November 2012.

10 Now take Major Street southbound (peek into Kosower Lane to see the colourful mosaic).

11 Then turn right on Ulster, left on Borden Street and right again on Vankoughnet Street.

Croft Street

12 You're in for a treat down Croft Street! There's the cute mural on a garage door, and the lovely porch covered with ivy but most of all, there's the spectacular mural about Toronto's great fire in 1904.

13 Before heading west, you might want to visit **Voodoo Child**, a tiny café east of Croft at 388 College.

14 Or there's **Q Space** (382), an original poetry café owned by publishers **Quattro Books**.

College Street

Funky **Aunties & Uncles** at 74 Lippincott is an all-day breakfast place with plenty of 50's paraphernalia.

15 There's lots of stuff to sift through in **Stephanian Pharmacy** (not a pharmacy!) at 412.

Then, there's **Manic Coffee** for your caffeine fix (426), followed by **Mars Food** (a classic greasy spoon!) and affordable **Nirvana** (dark medieval-like decor with a red twist).

16 **Sneaky Dee's** (431) is the place for nachos and beer and the option for bad girls! Bring your permanent pen to leave a quote on the washroom walls!

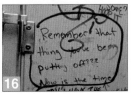

17 We've loved our late afternoon mojitos at **No One Writes to the Colonel**, a cool bar set in the 70s at 460 College, right next to amazing **Lilliput Hats**.

18 At Palmerston and College is a pocket of restaurants with lovely facades. Across the street, whimsical monkeys are attached to **Reiss Gallery**.

Kalendar's patio is very appealing (546 College) and colourful **Big Chill** (and **Little Dog** selling hot dogs in the back) is a must in the summer (367 Manning). **Ms. Emma Design** offers unique fashion at 543 College. **The Arthur** is a cute vintage shop (550).

Little Italy

19 **Motoretta** (554) is the first indication we're in **Little Italy**. **Café Diplomatico** (with its vast patio) is another clue at 594.

20 It is followed by multilingual **CHIN Radio**, west of **The Royal** cinema.

21 Gift shop **Red Pegasus** (628) is fun to visit, and so is shoe and accessory store **Balisi** (668).

22 Grace Street features an interesting monument to Johnny Lombardi.

23 From then on, Italian names florish: **Veni Vidi Vici**, **Vivoli**, **Sicilian Sidewalk Café**... But my heart goes to the awesome fish sandwiches of the tiny **Fish Store** (657, west of Grace).

24 I suggest you finish the stroll with a turn into Crawford (with interesting sidewalks) and a walk north on Grace for some Italian architectural detail.

MOUNT PLEASANT
INDULGING STROLL

You deserve a treat (don't you?)

I'll admit this walk is just an excuse to visit two French bakeries serving some of the prettiest pastries and best croissants in town: **Thobors** and **La Bamboche**. (There's no need to choose! Treat yourself in one of them and buy a take-out in the other.) **Mount Pleasant Village** has plenty of other goodies to offer: chocolates, vintage jewelry, high-end specialty food shops, garden decorations, doll house collectors' items, second-hand designer clothes. The street includes a cluster of fun places to shop for kids: **Mabel's Fables**, **Mastermind Toys**, **MiniGrid**, **Strategy** and two costume stores.

STROLL 16

Full loop:
3.6 km (55 min)

Shorter version:
The stroll's section along Mount Pleasant is a 1.3 km loop (20 min).

Game for more?
Mount Pleasant Cemetery Stroll (Stroll 9, p. 57) is accessible from a stair-case off Mount Pleasant, a 5-min walk south of Davisville Avenue.

Parking & TTC
• **Davisville Subway Station** is two blocks south of Belsize Drive on Yonge Street.
• There's an afford-able **Green P** at 650 Mount Pleasant (facing **Mastermind Toys**) but first try Thurloe Avenue which has no street parking restriction (take Belsize west of Mount Pleasant then turn right).

Other TIPS
• Many stores and res-taurants are closed on Mondays in this area.
• For the listings for the two independent theatres **Regent** (551 Mount Pleasant) and **Mount Pleasant** (675 Mount Pleasant), go to **cinemaclock.com**.

Thurloe Avenue

I always try to find a free parking space on Thurloe Avenue.

1 Walking up Thurloe to Servington Cres-cent, you can cross the park west of the **Church of Transfiguration**, to admire the ivy-covered side of the stone building by Manor East.

2 Then, I suggest you walk right on Manor to Mount Pleasant Road and have a bite at **Thobors** (627 Mount Pleasant, north of Manor).

Their tartines and croque-monsieurs are deli-cious. So is the rest.

Note that **Thobors** is closed on Mondays and Tuesdays. (If you plan to do this stroll on these days, or if you took the subway, go first to **La Bamboche**, at 4 Manor East. (It is open all week.)

North of Manor

Going northbound on Mount Pleasant, you'll pass **Mastermind Toys** on your right (639 Mount Pleasant).

3 It is followed by **Mabel's Fables**, on your left at 662. (They have a tiny adult nook and books for older kids as well as a French section on their second floor.)

4 If you don't need to shop for kids, you'll want to beeline to **D Davies Objets** (665) for some well curated vintage finds.

Look carefully and you'll notice very fancy necklaces in showcases. They're new creations made out of vintage never-used rhinestones.

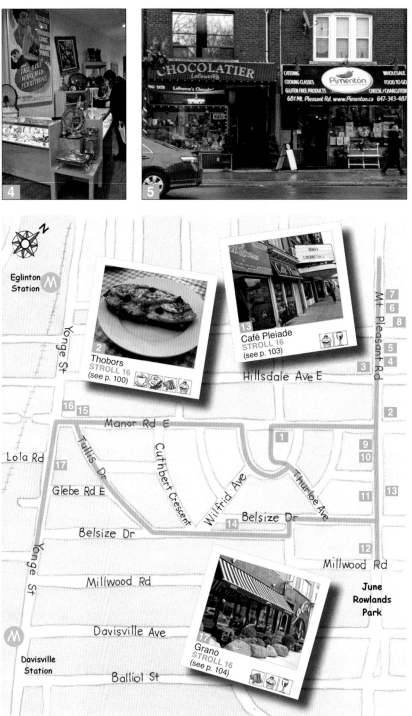

Thobors
STROLL 16
(see p. 100)

Café Pleiade
STROLL 16
(see p. 103)

Grano
STROLL 16
(see p. 104)

We found the staff very welcoming for a boutique selling one-of-a-kind pieces worth a few thousand dollars. (Note that I found myself a superb brooch from the 50s for $55.)

Past **Mount Pleasant** theatre (675 Mount Pleasant) are a few inspiring specialty shops.

5 There's **Pimentón** (681) carrying all kinds of goodies from Spain, including paëlla to go, adjacent to chocolatier **LeFeuvre's.**

Next door, **Candy's** is not about sweets. It's a costume shop (which used to be located further south, not too far from **Kids Costumes** (539).

Past well-stocked **Bernardi's Antiques,** we were greeted with a display of chess boards in **Strategy Games** (701).

6 They carry all kinds of strategy games and interesting books, such as *How to beat your dad at chess*.

They have a huge room set up for chess competitions. (The place is a not-for-profit, administered by the Chess'n Math Association promoting chess in schools.)

7 Further north, the gourmet grocery market **Culinarium** (705) sits pretty (they know how to set up a great window!). Nearby **Flaky Tart** (711) isn't bad either.

8 On our way back, we stopped at the tiny vintage jewelry store **The Bead Goes On** at 256 Soudan Avenue, just east of Mount Pleasant.

South of Manor

9   **Wildbird** (622 Mount Pleasant, on the west side) is my favourite destination on the street.

They offer such a fabulous assortment of home accessories, small furniture, candles, mirrors, lamps and all, that we tend to forget they also supply all kinds of bird seed.

10   **The Little Dollhouse Company** (612) is a must if you love miniatures. They have everything: books, wine glasses, tapestry, house molding, lamp fixtures for doll houses, etc. **MiniGrid** next door is another good stop for model cars.

11   For those who like to dig for treasures, there's designer resale **Act Two** (596), **Antiques on Mt. Pleasant** (562) and **Akladios Antiques** (558).

12   **Second Nature Boutique** (514) also features serious consignment designer items.

I liked the summer patio and mural of **Bread and Butter** (507).

13   Quaint **Café Pleiade** appealed to me (it would offer a nice dinner-and-a-movie combo with the independent theatre **Regent** next door (551).

But many other restaurant options caught my attention in the two blocks further north: **Boland's Open Kitchen** (575) with a fusion menu, **Florentia** (579), the two bistros **Mogette** (581) and **Simple Bistro** (619), and **Positano** (633). (Many are closed Sundays, Mondays and Tuesdays. **Boland's** and **Simple Bistro** are open for lunch.)

Glebe Manor Square

14 Next, I recommend you turn west on Belsize Drive to reach **Glebe Manor Square**, a long and narrow green space, with enough mature trees to provide welcomed shade during the summer and lovely fall colours in October.

Before Tullis Drive, have a peek on your left into the alley lined with black iron fences to see how nature fought its way through the links of the fence further south.

15 You'll find **La Bamboche** right where Tullis meets Manor East. Simple and pretty inside, its patio is quite cute in the summer. Their croissants are really good and their Japanese inspired French pastries, are almost too beautiful to eat.

Yonge Street

16 Just north of Manor is **Consign Toronto** (2095 Yonge), a consignment store packed with good finds.

17 In the next two blocks south on Yonge, you'll discover four fashion boutiques, three home decor stores and many shops with interesting facades such as **Five Doors North** at 2088 (with... five doors over their door) and **The Butcher's Son**'s grazing cow (2055). **Grano** (2035) includes a unique and colourful courtyard.

You can now return to Manor East, where you'll turn right, then right again on Servington Crescent, to Thurloe Avenue.

RONCESVALLES
REVAMPED STROLL

Roncesvalles is back on track!

It's been a rough road for the businesses along Roncesvalles Avenue during lengthy street construction which caused many of them to close. This made a decent stroll impossible for visitors. But those days are over. Last summer, we could admire the design of the new bike-friendly side road and enjoy the patios of the survivors and newcomers on the street. Once again, it is a cool destination with the funky vibes of unique stores mixing with a few old-Europe Polish shops. As a bonus, this stroll explores the most interesting grid of back lanes, creating a village within **Roncesvalles Village**.

STROLL 17

Full loop:
5.5 km (1 hr 20 min)

Shorter version:
If you stick to Roncesvalles, it's a 3.1 km stroll (45 min). Add the Sorauren Avenue section and it will be 4 km long (1 hr).

Game for more?
At the foot of Roncesvalles, west part of **Beaty Boulevard Parkette**, you'll find a footbridge running over the Gardiner, giving you access to the waterfront.

Parking & TTC
• **Dundas West Subway Station** is a 6-min walk from Roncesvalles and Dundas West intersection.
• The streetcar **#504** runs along Roncesvalles.
• There's lots of street parking after 10 a.m. east of Roncesvalles.

Other TIPS
• **Hugh's Room** (2261 Dundas W., just north of Roncesvalles) is a live music venue and a good restaurant (**hughsroom.com**).
• **The Revue** is a not-for-profit cinema at 400 Roncesvalles (**revuecinema.ca**).

Sorauren Avenue

1 I love starting this stroll along quaint Sorauren Avenue, using it as an excuse to have a hardy breakfast at **Mitzi's Café** (100 Sorauren at Pearson Avenue). There's something about this mischievous café that simply puts me in good spirits.

2 As you walk north on Sorauren, look up to see the architectural details.

3 You'll pass by two cafés. There's unassuming **Baluchon** (221 Sorauren, at Wright Avenue) and airy **Sunny Joe's Coffee** (250 Sorauren) further north, at Fermanagh.

4 Facing **Joe's** is **Charles G. Williams Park**. Walk into this little L-shaped park to see the large mural on the back wall. You can then exit onto Wright Ave., to your right.

Keep going west on Wright to reach Roncesvalles Avenue.

5 I really like how **Fern Avenue Public School** decorated its schoolyard with kid-made leaves and butterflies.

Roncesvalles

At Roncesvalles, you'll find a most colourful mural of the #504 streetcar line.

Each business along the main street has its own personality, which gives this neighbourhood its eclectic charm.

6 Northbound, you'll see slick **Lit Espresso Bar** (221), with dramatic lighting over the shiny coffee machine. You'll then have your first glimpse of the new bike lane system.

Past **St. Vincent de Paul Catholic Church**, with the imposing columns, take the time to peek inside **Smock Café** at 287 Roncesvalles. This unique drop-in centre for kids/restaurant is so creative, it makes you want to start doing crafts on the spot. (It is filled with whimsical details.)

7 Beyond Goeffrey Street, there's **Dressers** (307), a clothing store with an original facade and **Another Story Bookshop** (315), a quaint bookstore with a mission. **Mabel's Bakery** (323) with its striped awning also has curb appeal (and scrumptious treats to take out).

Mitzi's Café
STROLL 17
(see p. 106)

Cherry Bomb Coffee
STROLL 17
(see p. 110)

Hey!
STROLL 17
(see p. 110)

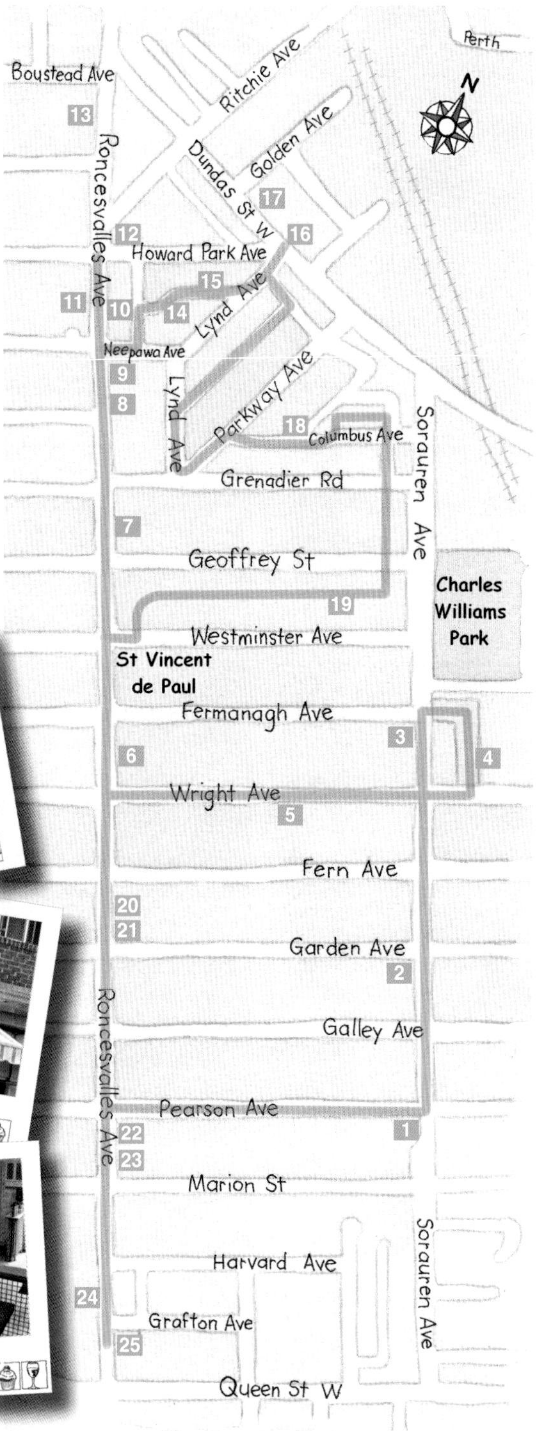

At **Fat Cat Wine Bar** (331, past Grenadier Road), the hidden patio in the backyard is the main attraction. This would be the spot for a late afternoon drink in the summer.

8 The **Chocolateria** (361) carries plenty of sweets while **Green Light District** (365) features a different kind of treats I'd love to take home: amazing pieces of furniture. **Fetch**, the canine shop next door, has the loveliest sign (I think I once saw the dog who inspired it sitting by the door).

9 The corner store at Neepawa is always flanked with plants.

10 In the next block, **Bead Junction** (389), new and used books at **She said boom!** (393), designer clothes at **Fresh Collective** (401) and gift shop **Scout** (405) are fun to sift through.

11 Across the street is the independent cinema **The Revue** (400). Check their programs. Last time I checked, they offered a very interesting concept: Epicure's Revue (featuring films about food or wine, with free samples from local merchants).

12 Just before Ritchie Avenue is **Maggie's Farm** (431), an irresistible vintage store filled with nooks to explore.

13 Thanks to an open house in the fall, I could see that the intriguing art on **Écouter Art Bar's** front yard at 462 is nothing to the cool bohemian installations in their backyard. You might want to check if it has finally opened.

The building at 459 is quite colourful as well. The unique workshop which sat next to it (**Marie Cla Ro**, making bags out of... car upholstery) has just moved closer to Ottawa.

Lanes stroll

I suggest you take this stroll into the labyrinth of Roncesvalles' alleyways. I was seduced by the small village feeling in the triangle grid south of Dundas West.

To better enjoy it, return to Neepawa Avenue and turn east, then take the first lane on your left and the first on your right. **14** You'll see a line-up of symmetrical garages. Expect a blue wave around the corner.

15 When you exit the alley, turn around to see the pretty houses on each side of the lane.

16 Turn left at Lynd Avenue. The intersection at Dundas West is charming. You'll see the funky mural *The Winds Are Changing* on your left (there's more around the building, including a tornado!). Overlooking it, across the street, is **Belljar Café** (2072 Dundas W.).

17 If you're into stained glass, you've got to visit **A.J. Stained Glass Supply** a bit further west at 2108 Dundas West.

Back on Lynd, take the first lane on your left, then walk into the first lane on your right.

18 Walk left around the corner onto Parkway, then take the first right into Columbus. Keep your right. You'll meet a dead-end in a cute nook.

12

13

14

14

15

16

15

16

17

18

18

The path will take you to **Columbus Parkette**. Turn right into the lane with the colourful garage doors.

This lane intersects Columbus Avenue. It also crosses Geoffrey Street.

19 Then take the long alleyway right after Geoffrey. (I found this circuit lively with people walking and kids biking.)

At the end, turn left onto Westminster Avenue and go back to Roncesvalles.

Of all the rest of the great places to discover down the street, I have favourites:

20 **Sweetpea's** (163), a flower shop with great gift section in the back and backyard.

21 The mural on **Solarski Pharmacy** at Garden Avenue (where you can spot a depiction of the church across the street).

22 The clothing shop **Frock** (97) and **Hey!** at 91 (with an interesting split-level layout).

23 When standing by **Cherry Bomb Coffee** (79) you can see the lake shining in the background down the street.

24 **Jewel Envy** (151 Marion Street at Roncesvalles) and **Mrs. Huizenga's** at 28 Roncesvalles, one block south across the street, both nicely end your shopping experience on this stroll (one, featuring the designs of artisan jewelers, and the other filled with original vintage finds).

25 **Grafton Park**, in the last block before Queen Street West, features a naive mural of the old Sunnyside amusement park.

Just the right mix

This stroll is part **Bloor West Village** (for some fun window shopping) and part **Swansea** (for a sneak into a lovely residential area). The mix of businesses on Bloor Street West between Jane Street and Runnymede Road indicates a dynamic local life, with enough interesting stores, restaurants and patios to satisfy outsiders. The hilly roads in **Swansea** offer a unique panorama. You'll find a few staircases along the way to explore intriguing nooks and crannies. You can end this stroll with a stop at **Max's Market** for some original take-out (to make up for the time you won't have spent preparing dinner).

STROLL 18

Full loop:
4.2 km (1 hr 05 min)

Shorter version:
For a 3.1 km stroll (45 min), don't cross S. Kingsway. Instead, walk north on it and turn right on Armadale Avenue all the way up to Bloor where you'll turn east to finish the loop.

Game for more?
Old Mill River Stroll (Stroll 10, p. 63) is .5 km north of Bloor (at the end of Old Mill Dr.).

Parking & TTC
• Exit at **Jane** or **Runnymede Subway Stations**.
• I usually find free street parking on Armadale Avenue.

Other TIPS
• **Humber Cinemas** (2442 Bloor W.) is located just west of Jane St., north side. See **humbercinemas. com** for their listings.
• The **Village Playhouse** (2190E Bloor W.) is a theatre run by volunteers, offering a wide range of professional plays. To find out what play is currently performing, visit **villageplayers.net**.

Willard Gardens

Willard Gardens is such a lovely street that I recommend trying to find street parking here to start the stroll (otherwise, Amadale Avenue will do).

1 The street dead-ends in **Willard Gardens Parkette**, with a long staircase.

2 In its elbow, you'll find another staircase leading up to a steep cliff to Yule Avenue.

Walk down Windermere Avenue and turn right at Rambert Crescent.

3 Where the street turns, you'll see a little clearing. This is public space. Walk into it for a surprising panorama of the rooftops of the properties down below.

Morningside Avenue

4 At Morningside Avenue, turn right. This street runs towards S. Kingsway. As you walk downhill, you'll have another great view.

This part of town truly is impressive with all the hilly terrain!

Morningside continues on the other side of S. Kingsway, where it slowly climbs up a ravine.

5 The street ends at a staircase going up to Riverside Drive, along the black iron fence of a gorgeous house.

Riverside Drive

6 Walk left on Riverside Drive and take the first street on your right, Riverside Trail. At the dead-end, you'll find stairs leading to the other side of Riverside Trail (also a dead-end road).

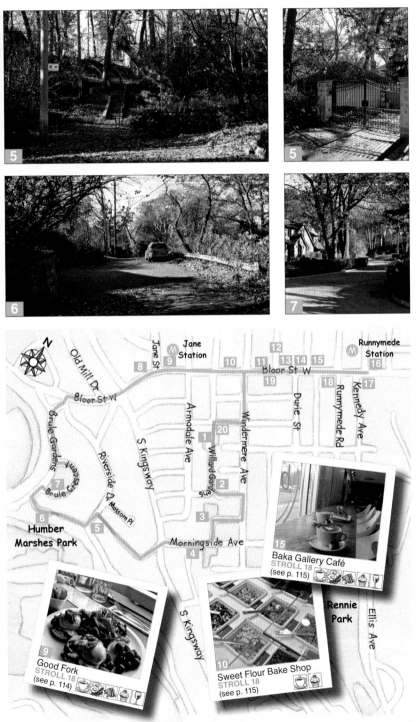

Baka Gallery Café
STROLL 18
(see p. 115)

Good Fork
STROLL 18
(see p. 114)

Sweet Flour Bake Shop
STROLL 18
(see p. 115)

Brule Gardens

Turn right at Brule Gardens. With all the trees, it does feel a bit like the country.

7 I suggest you walk up Brule Crescent and resume your stroll northbound on Brule Gardens.

You'll soon reach Bloor Street West.

Bloor Street West

The section of Bloor West, between Riverside Drive and Riverview Gardens, is not really interesting. (But aren't you glad you got to visit Swansea residential area?)

8 **Humber Cinemas** is in the next block (2442 Bloor W.). It is located near the gorgeous **Earth** (2448 Bloor W.). I'd love to have a bite and a drink on this restaurant's rooftop patio on a warm summer evening.

9 Past the pretty fountain, at Jane and Bloor West, the **Good Fork** (2432 Bloor W.) caught my attention with its red velvet pancakes (they open at 9 a.m.).

The entrance to **Jane Subway Station** on Bloor (by **Coffee Time** at 2424 Bloor W.) is unique, adorned with naive murals.

The gift shop **Quipus Crafts** at 2414 Bloor W. and adjacent **Coffee Tree Roastery** (serving breakfast and lunch) both have quaint charm.

Along the .6 km stretch between Armadale and Kennedy, I've noticed over a dozen fashion shops. It's an eclectic mix but you're bound to find one to your taste.

Tzat Z (2378 Bloor W., west of Willard Ave.) carries a wide selection of original (and comfortable) elegant clothes.

There's no seating at **Say Tea** (2362), but you might want to stock up on a vast choice of teas, coffee and related accessories.

10 At **Sweet Flour Bake Shop** (2352), they can cook a cookie for you under your nose, in a few minutes! You get to choose your dough and 2 mix-ins for $2.75. (Leaves a warm fuzzy feeling in your belly!)

11 The designer clothes in **Everhart** (2318) are to die for.

12 Peek into Durie Street north of Bloor as you go. It has a delightful small town appeal. See the whimsical decor inside the **Snappers Fish Market** (263 Durie St.).

13 In the next block, **Mer-ryGoRound** (2284) features urban chic collections in a narrow but deep space. Funkier **Trove** (2264) offers hip clothes, accessories and shoes.

14 **Accessorize Me** (2258) is jam-packed with fun bling (and pieces over $100 for fashionistas).

15 Beresford Avenue, north of Bloor Street, has character, thanks to **Zaza Espresso Bar** (also selling gelato) opposite to new **Baka Gallery Café** (as lovely outside with a great mural, as it is inside).

Simply Yours (2240) carries a line of bohemian chic clothes while **Cora Couture** (further east at 2236 Bloor West) features a more subtle palette of equally original fashion.

I was impressed by the selection of wider widths shoes at **Arka Shoes** (2196, just west of Kennedy Avenue).

Village Playhouse is a hidden venue below the street level at 2190E Bloor W.

16 When you reach the classy **Runnymede-Toronto Public Library**, cross Bloor and walk west-bound to explore the south side of the street.

17 On a warm summer day, I'd suggest you have a bite on the vast patio of trendy **Kennedy Public House** at Kennedy and Bloor. (In the winter, we've enjoyed a drink in their fancy decor.) A beer on the rooftop patio at **Swan & Firkin** (2205) would also do!

Nearby gorgeous shop **Write Impression** (2213) goes beyond its original passion for beautiful stationery.

18 The **Chapters** west of Runnymede is worth a visit. It used to be the Runnymede movie theatre, hence the unique architecture.

17 Steps (2241) is the clever name the friendly owners found to draw us into their warm Mediterranean restaurant, seventeen steps below.

19 I thought that **Sushi & Thai**'s decor (2279) was lovely, that **Bloor Meat Market** (2283) had great character and that **Max's Market** (2299) had a very appealing layout and a unique selection of prepared meals.

20 Finally, turn south at Windermere Avenue and right on Mayfield to access **Willard Gardens** (on your left hand side).

SUMMERHILL
UPTOWN GIRLS STROLL

Classy walk for classy girls

This stroll covers the prettiest stretch of Yonge Street, lined with home decor shops, specialty stores and restaurants, with a long list of superlatives. It includes Toronto's most beautiful **LCBO** store, **Patachou** and **Nadège** (serving some of the best French pastries in town), **The Shops of Summerhill** (the most chic cluster of fine food stores, under the black awnings of historic buildings), **The Rosedale Diner (**a landmark with the coolest facade) and **Reservoir Rosehill** (a park with the city's largest reflecting pool, most ambitious little garden and best access to the ravines).

STROLL 19

Full loop:
4 km (1 hr)

Shorter version:
If you limit your walk to Yonge Street and **Ramsden Park**, it's a 2.3 km stroll (35 min).

Game for more?
Rosedale Valley Fall Colours Stroll (Stroll 11, p. 69) is 10 minutes south of this stroll. (Off Yonge Street, turn east on Aylmer Ave., it becomes Rosedale Valley Rd.)

Parking & TTC
• Exit at **Summerhill** or **Rosedale Subway Stations**.
• There's a **Green P** on Price Street. In the afternoon, I usually try to get free street parking along Ottawa or Shaftesbury Avenues.

Other TIPS
• Many shops are closed on Sundays.
• To keep with the uptown girl's spirit, you could leave your car at **Mr. Shine** for detailing services while you do your walk in the neighbourhood (just drop in at 1128 Yonge). They start at $30.

Price Street
This is an uptown girl walk, so let's treat ourselves with paid parking at the **Green P** on Price Street, east of Yonge Street, shall we?

Walk south through the parking lot and turn right on Rowanwood Ave. to access a great block to start the stroll with a bite.

1 Right across the street, there's my favourite croissant bakery in Toronto, **Patachou Patisserie,** with seating available (1120 Yonge).

2 You're considering lunch? On a grey day, you could have a hot soup and great sandwich with a pint at **The Rebel House** at 1068 (this one will appeal to the bad girl side in you).

3 On a bright sunny day, I'd choose a table by the open bay windows at **Caffe Doria** (1094).

Then, I suggest you walk directly to **Rosehill Reservoir**, leaving the window shopping for later (that will be tough but you can try!). So, walk northbound on Yonge Street and turn right at Shaftesbury Avenue.

4 You'll turn left at the country-like intersection of Shaftesbury and Ottawa Street, then right at Summerhill Avenue.

Rosehill Reservoir
5 There's a path on your left running through a parkette. It leads to **Rosehill Reservoir**.

I decided to visit this park after noticing an intriguing blue water patch on Google Maps.

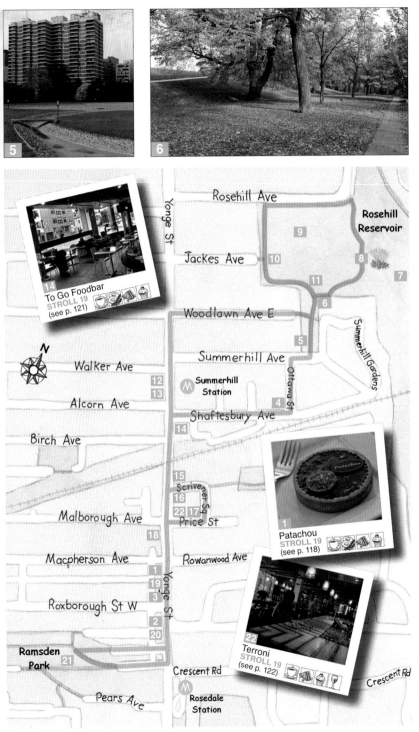

5

6

To Go Foodbar
STROLL 19
(see p. 121)

Rosehill Ave

Yonge St

Rosehill
Reservoir

9

Jackes Ave 10

8

11

7

6

Woodlawn Ave E

Summerhill Gardens

5

Summerhill Ave

N

Walker Ave

12

Summerhill
Station

13

Ottawa St

Alcorn Ave

4

Shaftesbury Ave

Birch Ave

14

15

Scrivener Sq

16

22 17

Malborough Ave

Price St

Patachou
STROLL 19
(see p. 118)

18

Macpherson Ave

Rowanwood Ave

1

Yonge St

19

3

Roxborough St W

2

20

Terroni
STROLL 19
(see p. 122)

Ramsden
Park

21

Crescent Rd

Crescent Rd

Pears Ave

Rosedale
Station

It turned out to be a huge reflecting pool composed of a series of irregular ponds, topped with a dramatic modern fountain.

6 Take the path to your right, along the hill, to enjoy this unique park.

7 If you kept walking, past the secluded playground, you'd access the nature trail to the **David A. Balfour Park**, further down into the ravine.

8 Climb up the hill before the playground and you'll see the lovely **Rosehill Garden**. (Make sure to close the iron gate to keep it dog-free!)

9 Then, walk towards the reflecting pool. It was built on top of the 53-million gallon underground reservoir. (It was in the open until 1966. Can you picture that?)

10 Finally, walk to Rosehill Avenue and follow the paved path around the park. Go up the staircase on the west side for a good view over the reservoir.

11 Then go down the stairs back into the parkette and turn right on Woodlawn Avenue East.

Yonge Street

Look north on Yonge and you'll see the banners of **The York School**, one of Toronto's trendy private schools. The window shopping may begin, as you stroll southbound on Yonge Street.

We passed a serious boutique filled with very expensive French antiques in favour of a whimsical little shop called **Room 2046** (1252 Yonge).

It sells an eclectic mix of gifts, clothing and books (plus you can order coffee and drink standing by the counter, as they do in Europe).

12 Beyond Walker Avenue, the real fun begins with **Absolutely North** (1236 Yonge), the bigger of two stores with the same name, also carrying bigger accessories and pieces of furniture (the other one is at 1132 Yonge). They feature a chic mix of antique and contemporary. **Alexia Von Beck**'s dresses at 1228 Yonge, past the contemporary **Muse Gallery**, would fit a decor created around the luxurious fabrics at **Department of Interiors** (1234 Yonge).

13 The **Châtelet** boutique (1226 Yonge) was a delight! Both whimsical and feminine, it features a vast collection of home accessories and furniture in a wide price range.

Next door, in captivating **L'Atelier**, we trade the Parisian ChiChi style for a more masculine world of exotic travels and smart adventures. The impressive display of a gorgeous row boat scull on the wall and ceiling definitely sets the tone.

As you stand at Shaftesbury, you'll get the best view down Yonge Street.

14 You'll also get this panorama if you sit by the windows inside **To Go Foodbar** at 133 Yonge, looking south over the **LCBO** (a good place for coffee and a casual light meal).

Scrivener Square

15 I love the Victorian feel of the steel viaduct further south. The entrance to **Timothy's** is right under that bridge.

Beyond lies a very nicely revamped section of Yonge, starting with the modern tipping water fountain of **Scrivener Square**, which feeds a stream running into reflecting pools along the **LCBO**. (Check the whimsical facade of **Rosedale Diner** across the street.)

The liquor store occupies what used to be **Summerhill Train Station**, featuring a 140-foot clock tower.

16 Next is the line-up of gourmet boutiques of **The Shops of Summerhill**, including the beautiful creations of **Nadège Patisserie** (1099 Yonge).

17 Around the corner is a high-end children's store with the best name: **Advice from a Caterpillar** (8 Price Street).

18 Among the rest of the best shops: jewelry and accessories at **Luxe and Found** (1134).

19 The bountiful selection of beautiful objects at **Putti** (1104).

20 Very cool home accessories and clothes at **Belle Époque** (1066), most original display of sample paint at **F & B** (1054) and irresistible dog toys at **Dogfather & Co.** (1007).

21 Make a little tour into **Ramsden Park**.

22 Then, how about a drink on the 2nd floor or on the rooftop patio of slick **Terroni** at 1095 Yonge?

Don't rush through this one!

This is the stroll to start on an empty stomach so you can first enjoy a bite at a local restaurant before touring the best cluster of vintage shops offering amazing collections of reclaimed material, unexpected finds and special creations made out of them. Many of the other stores you'll discover along Dundas West are true labours of love. Chances are your walk will have progressed so slowly that you'll feel the urge to stroll down the residential streets to burn off some calories before (or after) indulging again with **The Pie Shack**'s dessert, **Delight**'s artisanal chocolates or a latte at **Crema**.

STROLL 20

Full loop:
4.4 km (1 hr 05 min)

Shorter version:
If you stay on Dundas West, the stroll is 2.4 km long (35 min).

Game for more?
High Park Cherry Blossom Stroll
(Stroll 8, p. 51) is just 10 minutes south of Glendenan Avenue. It is an interesting walk, even when the cherry trees are not in full bloom.

Parking & TTC
• Bus line **#40** runs along Dundas Street West. Note that **High Park Subway Station** is a 20-min walk from Annette if you walk up Quebec Avenue.
• I don't usually have trouble finding free street parking along the streets north and south of Dundas West.

Other TIPS
• I heard only good things about the ambiance, food and great finds at the outdoor version of the **Junction Flea**, held every second Sunday from June to October (at the corner of Indian Grove and Dundas West).

East of Keele

1 What better way to start a girlfriends' outing than with a bite at **Cool Hand of a Girl** (2804 Dundas W.)? I don't know about their breakfasts but we ate some fantastic sandwiches there!

Junction Eatery (2790 Dundas W.) also looked very good. Note that the outdoor **Junction Flea** is held across from this restaurant on the second Sunday of every warm month. (I heard only good things about the flea market: great ambiance, great food, great finds.)

2 During a late afternoon outing in the area, my friends and I decided to treat ourselves with delicious margaritas at the Mexican restaurant **La Revolución** (2848 Dundas West).

If you don't aim for one of these places first, chances are you'll convince yourself later on not to walk "that far" and you'll miss out on them.

I usually park on quiet McMurray Avenue or Vine Avenue, north of Dundas West (finding free street parking is trickier east of Keele).

West of Keele

Once well fed, walk west-bound on Dundas to start your exploration of **The Junction**.

Make sure you have a peek at the little stretch just north on Keele. There used to be interesting stores there, which recently closed. Maybe they were replaced.

Cool Hand of a Girl
STROLL 20
(see p. 124)

Crema
STROLL 20
(see p. 127)

The Pie Shack
STROLL 20
(see p. 127)

3 Then, you've got to visit **Post and Beam** (2869 Dundas W.). They sell the kind of reclaimed architectural materials worth designing a room around. They sit right next to a funky bar called **Hole in the Wall**.

4 **Smash**, across the street, is a very deep store with high ceilings, filled with intriguing vintage finds. It is followed by **Cornerstore** which featured a clever display of chairs when we visited (don't miss their basement).

5 **Forever Interiors** (2903, past Mavety Street), features great furniture made out of reclaimed wood.

6 We were thrilled by the wide selection of used books at **Pandemonium** (2920) and the exhibition inside art supplies shop **ARTiculations** (2928).

7 **The Beet**, at the corner of Dundas and Medland, is an organic café serving delicious food. Its patio is lovely in the summer.

It is impossible not to be touched by the ingenuity of the stylish clothes at **IZ Adaptive**. They're beautiful and were created to be fully adaptable for people in a wheelchair (2955-B).

8 Further west, I fell in love with the warmth of the wooden Scandinavian items in the beautifully laid-out store **Mjölk** (2959).

9 Across the street, you'll see a space which looks like an old train station, adorned with a mural. (Can you see the little yellow horse in a box above groovy **Margret** bar?)

10 You'll see more railway references on the mural along Pacific Avenue. (**The Junction** gets its name because of CN and CP railways intersecting nearby.)

11 **Metropolis Living** (2989 Dundas W.) and **Eclectic Revival**, one block further (3075 Dundas W.), are two other fabulous places to admire creations reinventing vintage treasures.

12 On your way, you'll pass by **Delight** (3040 Dundas W.) selling delectable hand-made chocolates, and its neighbour **Junction Cheese** (set in a decor in true harmony with this hood).

13 Next time I go, I've got to try one of the breakfast sandwiches at **Locomotive** (3070 Dundas W.). I hope they still feature their cool collection of framed train-themed puzzles.

Quebec Avenue

Take some time to admire the crafts from local artists at **Wise Daughters** (corner of Dundas and Quebec).

14 Then, I recommend you walk down the line of charming houses and mature trees along Quebec Avenue. Note that you can grab a foamy latte at **Crema** before.

15 Or go one block down to **The Good Neighbour** on Annette Street. Decisions, decisions!

16 **The Pie Shack** stands at the corner of Annette and Clendenan, with its trademark giant pie. (We thought we wouldn't finish our quarter-of-a-pie piece but we gobbled it up!)

You'll see cute fish and turtle-shaped mosaics on the link fence of **Annette Street Public School** across the street before heading south on Clendenan Avenue.

Ravina Gardens

17 As you walk down the gentle slope, the trees will seem to get taller and the houses bigger until you reach **Ravina Gardens Park**, a cosy park with a playground nestled at the foot of some impressive backyards.

18 Clendenan then goes up and turns into Glendonwynne Road, forming one of Toronto's crossroads with the most curb appeal.

19 The charming landscape keeps unfolding as you stroll along Glendonwynne, around the grounds of **Humberside Collegiate Institute**. (Built in 1895, it is said to include five large mural paintings by Group of Seven Arthur Lismer in its auditorium.)

Malta Park

20 Back on Annette, turn left and return to Dundas Street along Clendenan Avenue to admire more houses.

21 I suggest you keep walking west on Dundas for one last interesting sight: **Malta Park**, the little triangular park straight from the 50's.

22 Returning eastbound, check the fashion store **Black Daffodil** (3097 Dundas W.). And next, isn't the facade of **Eclectic Revival** just perfect?

WYCHWOOD
COUNTRY STROLL
21

Toronto's countryside

This is a short but irresistible walk because it includes idyllic **Wychwood Park** (one of the few private streets in Toronto) and **Wychwood Barns Park** (one of the great examples of new architecture mixing with historic buildings). Add to this a soupçon of France, thanks to French bakery **Pain Perdu**, a bit of bohemian flair with **Gypsy Found Objects** vintage store, some funky vibes at **The Stockyards** smokehouse, Mediterranean tapas at **Mezzeta** and margaritas at **El Rincón**'s Mexican patio, all within a few blocks along St. Clair West, and you get quite a neighbourhood stroll.

STROLL 21

Full loop:
2.9 km (45 min)

Shorter version:
The tour of **Wychwood Park** from the gates is just 1 km (15 min).

Game for more?
The Casa Loma Staircase Stroll (**Stroll 22**, p. 135) is .9 km east of **Wychwood Park**'s street entrance, off Davenport Road.

Parking & TTC
• Christie Street is a 12-min walk from **St. Clair West Subway Station**. Streetcar **#512** runs along St. Clair Street West.
• You will find free street parking on Christie by **Artscape Wychwood Barns**.

Other TIPS
• **Artscape Wychwood Barns** is set in the former Wychwood TTC streetcar yard.
• A good article by Malcolm Johnston (Jan. 22, 2011 in the *National Post*) confirms that even though **Wychwood Park** is a private street, its residents are welcoming to visitors (... in case you were wondering).

St. Clair West

You should easily find free street parking on Christie Street, near **Artscape Wychwood Barns**.

If you don't feel like eating right away, start the walk by crossing the **Barns Park** to Wychwood Avenue and down into **Wychwood Park**. But I suggest you first walk north on Christie, to St. Clair.

One of my favourite French bakeries, **Pain Perdu,** being in the neighbourhood (736 St. Clair W.), means I prefer to start the stroll with breakfast at this place.

1 Across the street from the **Starbucks** is **World Class Bakers**. I bought a selection of their small cookies to take home and we really liked them.

2 Try **Pain Perdu**'s scrumptious French toast. (They also do a serious Croque-Monsieur!)

Passing by **The Rushton** further west at 740 St. Clair W., my friends and I agreed that we'd love to try their trio of burgers and great salads for lunch in the near future. And we did!

3 It faces **St. Matthew's United Church**, topped with an interesting bell tower.

4 Next, I like to walk straight to **Gypsy Found Objects** at 762 St. Clair W. (pace yourself because it only opens at 11 a.m.). Everything in this shop is top quality and beautifully laid out. They offer a mix of new and, as they put it, reclaimed, repurposed, curated vintage and antique.

Pain Perdu
STROLL 21
(see p. 130)

The Stockyards
STROLL 21
(see p. 132)

Hillcrest
Park

El Rincón
STROLL 21
(see p. 132)

5 **EcoExistence** nearby (766 St. Clair W.) sells all kinds of eco friendly products.

6 **Ferro**, the restaurant across from **Gypsy** also felt bohemian chic to us, with its eclectic mix of light fixtures, painting on the ceiling and dark tones.

We returned there on another occasion to have dinner and everything was delicious and well presented.

7 I found out that **Noir Coffee and Tea** (701) belongs to **Gypsy**'s owners. There's indeed a connection between the colour palette and the attention to details in both places.

The café features a cute Japanese alcove where I insisted we sit for tea. Bad call for my friend! She was wearing a skirt and could not find any dignified way to do it. (We laughed the whole time.)

8 I have also had the chance to have lunch at **The Stockyards** (699), a very funky joint where we had a great pulled pork sandwich.

9 Other fun lunch options in the next block are **Mezetta** (681) offering a tapas menu and **El Rincón** (653) with a cute patio where I'd like to have margaritas in the summer.

10 The café **CocoaLatte** (671) serves nice breakfasts and the boutique **Clay** (659) features interesting home and kitchen gadgets. Once again, these two businesses belong to the same owners.

11 They're followed by a little cluster of nice stores to browse through: **Kosoy & Bouchard** selling unique pieces in glass and porcelain, and the two clothing shops **La Boutique Parpar** and **One Girl Who...**

12 The quaint little bakery **Leah's** (621 St. Clair W.) is the last point of interest before heading south on Wychwood.

Wychwood Park

13 It will lead you past the open gates of **Wychwood Park**.

There are no sidewalks but this is a pedestrian friendly walk.

14 The country-like road forms a 1-km loop running around a large pond and it is at its best during the fall.

Cars used to be able to enter from Davenport Road on the south side but the residents have decided to fence it, leaving an opening for people (the kind of decisions you can make on a private street).

15 The sheltered tennis court nested in the ravine is not for the general public but you can watch a game from a bench.

Wychwood Barns

16 **Wychwood Barns** is set in the historic buildings of Wychwood TTC streetcar repair yard, hence the streetcar photos in the main barn.

17 As you walk towards Christie, you'll pass by the cute playground, the community garden and an off-leash dog park.

Move over Stairmaster!

For years, I visited **Casa Loma** with my kids without realizing Toronto's most impressive staircase lies at the foot of a little park just east of the castle. It offers a great view of Spadina Road... and of personal trainers torturing poor women huffing and puffing up and down the stairs, casually suggesting "One more, two steps" to the red-faced client as she runs by while he stands watching. No need to run if you don't want to but this stroll also includes the staircase under Spadina, the one down **Nordheimer Ravine**, two more around **Sir Winston Churchill Park**, and a chocolate treat.

Full loop:
4.8 km (1 hr 10 min)

Shorter version:
If you stick to the stroll section west of Spadina, taking the stairs up Spadina instead of pursuing **Roycroft Park**, it is 3.4 km (50 min).

Game for more?
The Wychwood Country Stroll
(Stroll 21, p. 129) is 1 km away (take Austin Terrace westbound to Bathurst, then Alcina Ave. (the second street north, to your left).

Parking & TTC
• Exit at **St. Clair West** or **Dupont Subway Stations**.
• It's hard to find street parking for more than 2 hours (but easier on the weekends). Parking lots at **Casa Loma** or **George Brown** cost around $8.

Other TIPS
• **Spadina House** was restored to its 1930's state. (The music room is gorgeous!) Closed on Mondays, it is open at least from 12 noon to 4 p.m. the rest of the week.

Macpherson Ave.
Most street parking spots around this stroll are good for two hours or less. So I prefer to play it safe and use the **George Brown College** parking lot, on Macpherson ($5/weekends and $8/weekdays to park from 6 a.m. to 6 p.m.).

1 If you're not willing to wait until you get to St. Clair Avenue to grab a coffee, you can get one at **George Brown** (at least between 7:30 a.m. and 2 p.m.) in their cute food court on Floor 2 of Building C near the bookstore. It's your chance to sneak around the campus.

I enjoyed the high ceiling with skylight near the information desk.

Baldwin Steps
2 Go north on Kendall (or Walmer Rd) then turn right on Davenport to access the **Baldwin Steps** reaching up to the small park by **Casa Loma**. Spadina spreading down below looks like a little Avenue des Champs-Élysées.

3 Up the staircase, you'll get a glimpse of the castle to your left and **Spadina Museum: House and Gardens** on your right.

Walmer Street
4 Walk up Spadina Road then turn left on Castle View Avenue. At the end of the street is the red facade of **Casa Loma's** coach house on Walmer Road.

5 Walk northbound on Walmer to access a cute little nook to your left, leading to Connable Drive.

To your right is the lovely Russel Hill Drive, which I recommend you explore on your way back from this loop.

Lyndhurst Avenue

Connable Drive is a quiet street meeting Lyndhurst Avenue where we can see a series of chic townhouses with what seems like their own private little street.

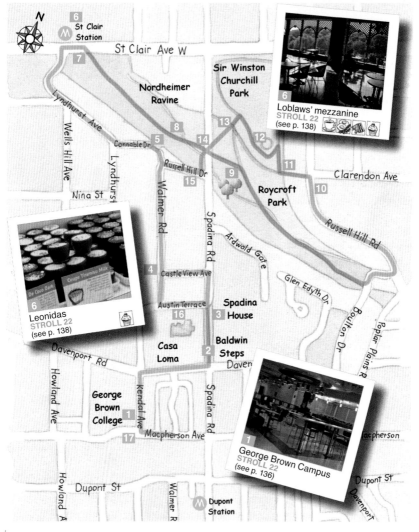

Loblaws' mezzanine
STROLL 22
(see p. 138)

Leonidas
STROLL 22
(see p. 138)

George Brown Campus
STROLL 22
(see p. 136)

St Clair Station

St Clair Ave W

Nordheimer Ravine

Sir Winston Churchill Park

Lyndhurst Ave

Wells Hill Ave

Connable Dr

Lyndhurst

Nina St

Russell Hill Dr

Walmer Rd

Spadina Rd

Clarendon Ave

Roycroft Park

Russell Hill Rd

Ardwold Gate

Glen Edyth Dr

Castle View Ave

Austin Terrace

Spadina House

Boulton Dr

Poplan Plains R

Davenport Rd

Howland Ave

Casa Loma

Baldwin Steps

Daven

George Brown College

Kendal Ave

Macpherson Ave

Spadina Rd

Macpherson

Howland A

Dupont St

Walmer R

Dupont Station

Dupont St

Davenport

I've not included it in the stroll but if you walk southbound on Lyndhurst, you'll be able to admire a few impressive houses nicely framed by mature trees.

Turning northbound on Lyndhurst, you'll pass by the cute **Wells Hill Park**, then you will face the **Forest Hill Loblaws**.

You can grab a bite and good coffee made with their special Swiss machine, by the entrance off St. Clair West, and take it to their second floor.

6 The mezzanine in this **Loblaws** (which opens at 7 a.m.) is lined with bay windows and offers a very pretty view of the trees in **Nordheimer Ravine**.

At the parking level, you'll find **Leonidas**, selling fresh Belgian chocolates. I suggest you treat yourself with a few chocolates to savor at the end of your stroll.

Nordheimer Ravine

7 You can access the ravine from a staircase at the lights across from Loblaws. **Nordheimer Ravine** includes a main gravel trail and a few dirt side trails.

Don't worry, you can't get lost!

8 You'll pass a small marsh before reaching a cobblestone section. You're now under the Spadina Road viaduct.

At this point you could climb up the staircase to walk back to **Casa Loma** if you're short of time.

Otherwise, push it to **Roycroft Park**.

Roycroft Park

9 Keep following the path into **Roycroft Park** (don't go up the hill to your left yet, the loop will take you there a bit later). The sinuous dirt trail will lead you into **Glen Edyth Wetland**.

You can sometimes see volunteer gardeners clearing the bush. They've done a great job at rejuvenating the area (you should have seen the place 10 years ago).

Now and then, you can see the backyards of some serious properties (always a bonus, isn't it?).

At the end of the park, turn left to Russell Hill Road. Note that you could also cross Boulton Drive and keep walking up little **Poplar Plains Parkette**, then turn left on Russel Hill.

Russell Hill Road

Russell Hill is a beautiful road all the way up to St. Clair West. (Before starting the stroll, I like to drive down this street to try my luck at snapping one of the spots in the section south of Clarendon Ave. where one can park after 9 a.m.)

10 Russell Hill is especially charming at Clarendon, with a stone wall on one side and a picture-perfect cottage-like house by the path leading to the park.

Sir Winston Churchill

11 The fork to your right will take you to the staircase leading to the main plateau of **Sir Winston Churchill Park** (also an off-leash dog park).

12 Take a couple of minutes to admire the view over the valley. Then follow the circular path to the small yellow house.

13 Go down the staircase and walk towards the viaduct.

14 You'll see stone steps under the bridge, climbing up to the west side of Spadina Road. Whenever I go up that staircase, I feel like I'm walking amidst some mysterious Indonesian ruins. (OK, maybe I have too much imagination...)

Russel Hill Drive

15 Up the stairs, take Russel Hill Drive, the first street to your right off Spadina Road.

Hard to believe we're in Toronto, isn't it? The tiny road is wide enough to let one car go at a time and runs under an arch of greenery. It takes you to Walmer Road.

Casa Loma

16 Stroll southbound on Walmer then turn left on Austin Terrace to walk along **Casa Loma**, for a good look at Canada's largest house, with 98 rooms, which owner Sir Henry Pellatt had to let go in 1924 (due to a financial hardship after WW1).

17 Then, it's the last staircase back to your starting point, and one last stop (if you're doing this stroll on a weekday between 9 a.m. and 5 p.m.): **Julia West Home**, the great home decor store filled with savvy displays (140 Kendal Avenue).

HIGH PARK
FITNESS STROLL
23

Urban life has its ups and downs

West of **High Park**, the streets are lovely... and steep. It's the perfect terrain for a good fitness walk: You'll be so busy admiring the properties, you won't even feel your muscles burning, but they will. (Of course, you don't need to rush through it.) This stroll will take you up and down every beautiful stretch of sloped trail or road I could find, including the northwest dirt path in **High Park**. Note that it's not all hard work. This walk will also lead you to the tranquil oasis of **West Pond**, closer to The Queensway, and will give you the choice of two great cafés on Bloor Street: **Red Bean** and **Café Novo**.

STROLL 23

Full loop:
5.7 km (1 hr 25 min)

Shorter version:
If you stick to the north of Morningside Avenue, it will be a 3.1 km walk (45 min).

Game for more?
High Park Cherry Blossom Stroll (Stroll 8, p. 51) continues where **Stroll 23** leaves **High Park**, by **Wendigo Pond**. Interesting walk even if the trees aren't in bloom.

Parking & TTC
• Exit at **High Park Subway Station**.
• I can usually find free street parking along Wendigo Way. Otherwise, I like to park along Dacre Crescent, west of Ellis Park Road.

Other TIPS
• You might want to drive to gourmet emporium **Cheese Boutique** in the area at 45 Ripley Avenue. They've got the best of everything! Take South Kingsway northbound from The Queensway and turn into the first street to your right. (It's a 15-min walk from **West Pond**.)

Wendigo Way

The streets just west of **High Park** are all one-of-a-kind but Wendigo Way is unique. I always try to find free street parking there first.

1 Then, I walk up the metal staircase to Bloor Street and to the right to grab myself a coffee at **Café Novo**, across the street (just past Parkside Gardens, where you'll find an entrance to **High Park Subway Station**).

High Park

2 Back to the stairs, and down, turn into the trail entering **High Park**.

3 Take the first fork to your right to follow the path running through the forest.

4 You'll eventually have the chance to turn right towards the pond, which you will pass to access Ellis Park Road.

Ellis Avenue

5 Ellis Park Rd. is a steep street with a good view of the pond on the left side.

6 It turns up into Morningside Ave.

7 At the Presbyterian church, walk southbound down Ellis Ave. You'll be able to admire serious real estate on the east side.

8 I suggest you stroll up Grenadier Heights to your left, for a lovely panorama on your way down towards Ellis Avenue, where you'll cross the street to the west side.

Keep going southbound along the pretty properties by the water.

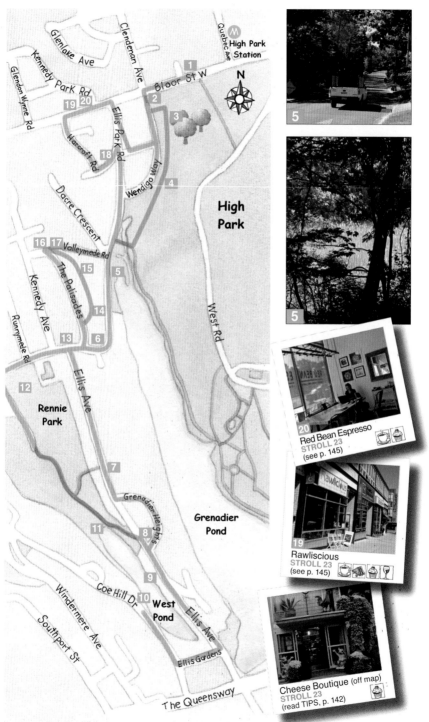

High Park Station

Glenlake Ave

Clendenan Ave

Quebec Ave

Kennedy Park Rd

Glendon Wynne Rd

1

Bloor St W

N

2

19 **20**

3

Ellis Park Rd

Harcroft Rd

18

Dacre Crescent

Wendigo

4

High Park

16 **17** Valleymede Rd

The Palisades

15

5

Kennedy Ave

14

West Rd

Runnymede Rd

13   **6**

Ellis Ave

12

Rennie Park

7

Grenadier Heights

Grenadier Pond

11   **8**

9

Windermere Ave

Coe Hill Dr   **10**   West Pond

Ellis Ave

Southport St

Ellis Gardens

The Queensway

Red Bean Espresso
STROLL 23
(see p. 145)

Rawliscious
STROLL 23
(see p. 145)

Cheese Boutique (off map)
STROLL 23
(read TIPS, p. 142)

West Pond

9 A bit further south, you'll have a better look at **West Pond** through the trees. A bench has been installed in the perfect spot. The waterfront houses across the pond look gorgeous, don't they?

With some luck, you'll catch sight of graceful swans.

At Ellis Gardens, turn right, and then right again on Coe Hill Drive to see what it looks like on the other side.

10 There's a little landscaped patch (featuring a bird house on a pole) with a nice view of the east bank of the pond.

Return to Ellis Avenue, walk northbound and look for some steps going down a trail in the grove on your left (near Grenadier Heights).

11 This will take you to lovely wetlands with a small bridge.

The trail continues north of the bridge. (After a rainfall, it could be muddy over a few metres but it gets better right after.)

You can take a right fork which will lead you to another little bridge, up some stairs and between two houses into Ellis Avenue.

I prefer walking straight to get to **Rennie Park**.

Rennie Park

Walk around the rink on your left when you access the park.

12 **Rennie Park** is very pretty on its western part by Rennie Terrace. I've seen families picnicking along Wallace Avenue (the park continues across the street).

Walk through the park to get to Morningside Avenue and turn right.

The Palisades

13 Past the church, you'll take your left on the street called The Palisades.

14 If you feel adventurous, turn in the first lane you'll see on your right (past the first house). It is lined with old garages and ends with a dirt path you can follow to your left.

15 The trail takes you along backyards under mature trees. (Sometimes, you'd really think that you're on private property but municipal signs are proof that this is a public passage.)

16 If you prefer, keep strolling up The Palisades. At the turn, take the staircase on your right.

17 Both ways lead to Valleymede Road.

Ellis Park Road

18 Back on Ellis Park Road, turn left for a last climb into the very pretty and very steep Olympia Avenue, on your left. Take Harcroft Road on your right to reach Bloor.

19 If you don't feel too sweaty, you might want to have a healthy bite at **Rawliscious** at 2122 Bloor St. West. It features a raw food menu (they have desserts too!).

20 Or there's **Red Bean Espresso**, a café with cool decor of reclaimed doors (2118 Bloor W.).

Then, walk east to Ellis Park Road and take the left fork running lower, to end this stroll. Good job!

A stroll on higher ground

Once you've done this stroll, you'll understand why they call it "Upper Beaches"! It is indeed a good climb to get there from **The Beach** neighbourhood and there's no better way to do it than through **Glen Stewart Ravine**, just south of **Upper Beaches**. Up on Kingston Road awaits well deserved treats: good coffee, creamy scones, family diners. (How about a beer with a dart game? A bit too rowdy?) On your way back into **The Beach**, the downhill walk takes you through lovely streets with enough cottage-like houses to remind you that it used to be the summer retreat for Torontonians.

Full loop:
4.9 km (1 hr 15 min)

Shorter version:
The stroll section covering **Glen Stewart Ravine** and Kingston Road is 2.4 km (35 min).

Game for more?
It would add 1.7 km (25 min) to this stroll if you continued south at the ravine's main staircase and through the park nestled between Glen Manor Dr. East and West to reach Queen Street, where **Pie Shack** (2305 Queen E.) awaits.

Parking & TTC
• The streetcar **#502** runs along Kingston Road.
• There's plenty of free street parking on MacLean Avenue and Pine Crescent. I also like to park near the ravine's entrance on Glen Manor Dr. East.

Other TIPS
• The **Fox Theatre** is an independent movie theatre located at 2236 Queen East (between Willow and Beech Avenues). Visit **foxtheatre. ca** for listings. They often do a 6:45 p.m. presentation.

Pine Crescent

1 Try to find street parking on MacLean Avenue, Pine Crescent or nearby Glen Manor Drive and start this stroll with a walk up the elegant pavement of Pine Crescent.

This S-shaped street is lined with beautiful properties.

2 On the way, peek west into tiny Pine Glen Rd. to see the pedestrian bridge running over the park.

3 Turn left on Balsam Avenue and look for the schoolyard. Across from it, you'll notice a discreet entrance to the ravine, between two houses.

4 This passage will take you to the new stairs (and a part of the ravine most visitors missed before because they tended to stick to the main path).

This is where you'll get the best panoramic view over the ravine.

Glen Stewart Park
If you haven't visited **Glen Stewart Park**'s ravine in the last year, you're in for a surprise! It's undergone major revitalization.

5 The new staircase is spectacular, the sort of addition you'd expect in a national park. This is what we get when talented urban planners are given a $1-million budget to improve a municipal ravine.

6 If you turned left at the foot of the stairs, you'd pass by a stream singing through pretty wetlands and you'd reach Glen Manor Dr. East. If you kept walking south, you'd see a gorgeous rockery right before Queen.

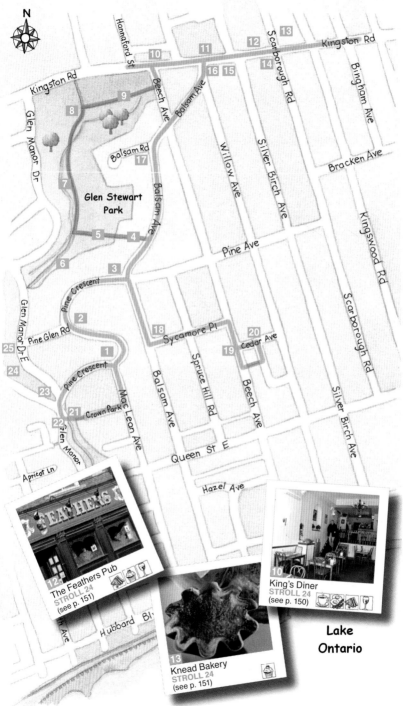

N

Hannaford St

Kingston Rd

Scarborough Rd

Kingston Rd

Bingham Ave

10

11

12

13

16 15

14

Beech Ave

Balsam Ave

Glen Manor Dr

Kingston Rd

8

9

Bracken Ave

Balsam Rd

17

Willow Ave

Silver Birch Ave

Kingswood Rd

Glen Stewart Park

7

5

4

Pine Ave

6

3

Pine Crescent

Glen Manor Dr E

Pine Glen Rd

2

18   Sycamore Pl

20   Cedar Ave

Scarborough Rd

1

19

25

24

Pine Crescent

Balsam Ave

Spruce Hill Rd

Beech Ave

Silver Birch Ave

23

Mac Lean Ave

21   Crown Park

22   Glen Manor

Queen St E

Apricot Ln

Hazel Ave

The Feathers Pub
STROLL 24
(see p. 151)

King's Diner
STROLL 24
(see p. 150)

Knead Bakery
STROLL 24
(see p. 151)

Hubbard Bl

Lake Ontario

7 Instead, I suggest you turn right on the boardwalk down the staircase. You'll walk up and down slopes under mature trees and come upon a fork where the trail starts to go up again. Both branches take you to Kingston Road.

8 The one straight ahead leads to a wooden staircase, the shortest route to the street. I suggest you embark on the path to your right. It will take you to Beech Avenue through a wilderness trail.

9 Further up, you'll have a good view of the ravine, way down below and over properties on the edge of the steep hillside. (This is one deep ravine!)

Once on Beech Avenue, turn left to access Kingston Road, which is the southern limit of **Upper Beaches**.

Kingston Road

Walk to Hannaford Street and work your way eastbound on the north side to explore Kingston Road.

10 First you'll see cute **Cobalt Gallery** (870A Kingston). Then **Objektkul** (882), featuring fantastic furniture made out of reclaimed materials, is next to **Custom Antique**.

King's Diner (906) is an old-fashioned family restaurant which seems much appreciated by locals.

Zilberschmuck (910) displays amazing silver jewelry.

11 Further east, **Trinity Gallery II** (920) offers a selection of home decor items while **Trinity Gallery** (926) focuses on clothing and accessories.

12 **Threads Lifestyle** (950 Kingston) and sport footwear **Keen** are neighbours to **The Feathers Pub** which offers a real pub experience, dart game and all.

13 **Knead Bakery** (around the corner at 283 Scarborough) is a place to stock up on baked goodies.

At Victoria Park Avenue, cross to the south side and walk westbound.

14 At the waterfall mural, there's **Savoury Grounds** (959 Kingston) a coffee roaster sitting next to **The Great Escape** secondhand bookstore.

15 The next block is the quaintest with **Neo** clothing store at 933, **Pegasus**, a little thrift shop with a mission, **Close to the Bone**, the meat shop next to **The Art of Cheese**.

16 Then, there's the mural on **Kumon** and **Mullins Irish Pub** at the corner.

Balsam Avenue

17 Walk southbound on Balsam Ave. (in the spring, the hedge past Balsam Rd. is spectacular).

18 Keep going down, past Pine Crescent and turn left on Sycamore Place.

19 Take Beech Avenue to your right and look for an intriguing little lane called Pine Terrace. It is an odd sidewalk crossing the backyards of the houses facing Cedar Avenue.

20 Turn left at the lane for a view reminiscent of a small village. Then it's left again on Cedar to backtrack to Pine Crescent.

21 to **25** Note that you can access the park from the stairs at the foot of Crown Park Road.

This looks good...
Let's go for a walk!

Decisions, decisions...

- Do you need a **caffeine fix**?
- Are you hungry for **breakfast**?
- Do you want to have **lunch**?
- Do you deserve a **treat**?
- How about an **afternoon drink**?

Let the following suggestion
index inspire you.

SUGGESTION INDEX

SUGGEST

ION INDEX

Do you want to find a stroll around a good place
for your caffeine fix?

Snakes & Lattes
STROLL 1
(see p. 10)

On Bloor W., west of Markham
*Toronto's board game café!
(They serve alcohol.)* Open daily
at least from 11 a.m. to midnight.

Ideal Coffee
STROLL 2
(see p. 19)

At Ossington & Foxley
*Great coffee in laid-back ambi-
ance.* Open weekdays at 8 a.m.
and at 9 a.m. on weekends.

Foodwares Market
STROLL 3
(see p. 22)

In The Bay's lower level
Lovely urban Canadiana decor
Open weekdays at 7:30 a.m., 9:30
a.m. Saturdays, 11:30 a.m. Sundays

SJCB
STROLL 3
(see p. 26)

In underground PATH
Superb coffee, cool counter
Open weekdays only, 7 a.m. to
4 p.m.

Red Rocket
STROLL 4
(see p. 32)

At Wellesley & Homewood
*Good coffee and tasty treats in
a cool urban decor*
Open daily from 7 a.m. to 6 p.m.

Aroma Espresso Bar
STROLL 7
(see p. 48)

In Forest Hill, on Spadina
*Very slick decor, great coffee and
food.* Open weekdays from 7 a.m.
and from 8 a.m. on weekends.

Café Novo
STROLL 8
(see p. 55)

By High Park
Lovely window counter
Open weekdays 7 a.m. to 7 p.m.,
weekends at least 9 a.m. to 6 p.m.

Balzac's Coffee
STROLL 11
(see p. 74)

In Toronto Reference Library
Balzac's trademark roast
Open weekdays from 7 a.m. (Sat-
urdays 8 a.m., Sundays 10 a.m.).

Remarkable Bean
STROLL 12
(see p. 78)

On Queen E., east of Beech
Great coffee and salty muffins
Open from 7 a.m. to 10 p.m.
(closed on Sundays).

"Many coffee shops can fix great chai lattes
for tea lovers."

Broadview Espresso
STROLL 13
(see p. 85)

Crema
STROLL 13
(see p. 86)

Sam James Coffee Bar
STROLL 15
(see p. 94)

At Broadview & Pretoria
Great out-of-the-way local café
Open weekdays 7 a.m. to 7 p.m., weekends at least 9 a.m. to 5 p.m.

On busy Danforth
Love to sit at the window counter!
Open 7:30 a.m. to 8 p.m., opens at 8 a.m. on Sundays.

On quiet Harbord
Superb coffee, cool counter
Open weekdays 7 a.m. to 6 p.m., weekends at least 9 a.m. to 5 p.m.

Lit Espresso Bar
STROLL 17
(see p. 106)

Cherry Bomb Coffee
STROLL 17
(see p. 110)

Coffee Tree Roastery
STROLL 18
(see p. 114)

On Roncesvalles, north of Wright
Shiny red coffee machine
Open weekdays 7 a.m. to 6 p.m., 8 a.m. to 6 p.m. on weekends.

On Roncesvalles
Good coffee. Love the cherry!
Open weekdays 7 a.m. to 6 p.m., weekends at least 9 a.m. to 6 p.m.

On Bloor W., east of Jane
Roasting their own coffee
Open 7 a.m. to 7 p.m. (10 a.m. to 5 p.m. on Sundays).

Baka Gallery Café
STROLL 18
(see p. 115)

The Good Neighbour
STROLL 20
(see p. 127)

Red Bean Espresso
STROLL 23
(see p. 145)

Lovely decor on Beresford
Very friendly, very yummy!
Opens at 8 a.m. Monday to Saturday and at 9 a.m. on Sundays.

At Quebec & Annette
Cool building, quaint ambiance
Open daily from 7 a.m. to 7 p.m.

Reclaimed vintage on Bloor W.
Decor as cool as staff... and serving gelato. Open weekdays at 8:30 a.m., 9 a.m. on weekends.

"All the restaurants serve coffee but it's not always memorable. These coffee shops will do the trick."

Do you want to find a stroll around a good place
for decadent treats?

Hodo Kwaja
STROLL 1
(see p. 14)

On Bloor W., east of Manning
Walnut cakes, thick pancakes
Open daily from 9 a.m. (closed on Sundays).

Caldense Bakery
STROLL 2
(see p. 16)

West of Ossington
Best Portuguese custard tarts
Open daily, very, very early!
(Some mornings from 5 a.m.)

Petit Four
STROLL 3
(see p. 24)

Catering counter on the PATH
We love their dessert shots.
Open weekdays 7:30 a.m. to 8 p.m. (Fridays, closes at 3 p.m.)

Dutch Dream
STROLL 7
(see p. 46)

On Vaughan, north of St. Clair W.
Most whimsical ice cream shop
Open daily from 12 noon in summer and from 5 p.m. in winter.

XoxoCava
STROLL 9
(see p. 61)

On Yonge, north of St. Clair
Chocolate, hot chocolate...
Open from 10 a.m. (closed on Sundays and Mondays).

Ma Maison
STROLL 10
(see p. 66)

On Bloor W., east of Royal York
Fine French pastries, cute place
Open from 8 a.m.to 6 p.m.
(closed Sundays and Mondays).

Swirl Cup
STROLL 10
(see p. 66)

Near Humber River
Scrumptious cupcakes
Open daily from 11 a.m. (from 12 noon on Sundays).

Zane Patisserie
STROLL 12
(see p. 76)

Near Woodbine Park
Lovely French pastries
Open daily from 7:30 a.m. to 5:30 p.m.

Athens Pastries
STROLL 13
(see p. 86)

On Danforth, east of Logan
Honey balls... Can't stop at one!
Cute decor in the back. Open daily from 9 a.m. to 11 p.m.

"Spread the joy. Bring some to your loved ones!"

DT Bistro
STROLL 15
(see p. 96)

La Bamboche
STROLL 16
(see p. 100)

Thobors
STROLL 16
(see p. 100)

Very classy on Harbord
Spectacular desserts!
Open from 10 a.m. (closed
Mondays and Tuesdays).

Off Yonge at Manor
*Beautiful and original pastries,
very good croissants.* Open
daily 8 a.m.to at least 9 p.m.

On Mount Pleasant
Classic French pastries. Yum!
Open 7:30 a.m. to at least 5:30 p.m.
(closed Mondays and Tuesdays).

Sweet Flour Bake Shop
STROLL 18
(see p. 115)

Patachou
STROLL 19
(see p. 118)

Nadège Patisserie
STROLL 19
(see p. 122)

On Bloor W., east of Willard
Made-to-order cookie in minutes!
Open weekdays 7 a.m. to 9 p.m.
(weekends, 9 a.m. to at least 7 p.m.).

French flair on Yonge
Lemon tart, rasberry tart...
Open weekdays 8 a.m., Saturday
8:30 a.m. (closed on Sundays).

On Yonge, north of Price
Pastries as gorgeous as delicious
Open from 9 a.m. to at least 6
p.m. (closed on Mondays).

Delight
STROLL 20
(see p. 127)

The Pie Shack
STROLL 20
(see p. 127)

Pain Perdu
STROLL 21
(see p. 130)

On Dundas West
Beautifully crafted chocolates
Open daily at least from 11 a.m.
to 8 p.m.

Sitting pretty on Annette
*Quarter-of-a-pie pieces, lovely
decor.* Open from 11 a.m. to 8 p.m.
(closes at 5 p.m. on Sundays).

On St. Clair W., east of Rushton
*Time to try a millefeuille! Or the
thick Pain Perdu!* Open daily
from 8 a.m. to 6 p.m.

"Many decadent shops do not offer seating."

Do you want to find a stroll around a good place
for breakfast?

Future Bistro
STROLL 1
(see p. 10)

On Bloor W. at Brunswick
All-day breakfast, great patio...
and cheesecake! Open daily
from 8 a.m.

Insomnia Cafe
STROLL 1
(see p. 12)

On Bloor W., east of Bathurst
Try the French toast!
Open weekdays at 10 a.m. and
at 9 a.m. on weekends.

Lakeview Restaurant
STROLL 2
(see p. 18)

On Dundas West
Retro booths, great patio, they
serve deep fried Mars bars!
Open daily, 24 hours.

Marché Restaurant
STROLL 3
(see p. 25)

Near Brookfield Place arches
Great bowl of café au lait!
Open daily from 7:30 a.m. to at
least 11 p.m.

Chew Chew Diner
STROLL 4
(see p. 32)

At Carlton & Bleecker
All-day breakfast with vast
menu. Open daily from 8 a.m.
to 8 p.m.

Starving Artist
STROLL 5
(see p. 38)

At Lansdowne & Paton
Quality waffles and superb
coffee. Open daily from 9 a.m.
to 6 p.m.

Aroma Espresso Bar
STROLL 7
(see p. 48)

In Forest Hill, on Spadina
Very slick decor, great coffee and
food. Open weekdays from 7 a.m.
and from 8 a.m. on weekends.

Aunties & Uncles
STROLL 15
(see p. 97)

Off College, on Lippincott
Funky place, funky vibe from
the 50's, nooks and crannies.
Open daily from 9 a.m. to 3 p.m.

Mars Food
STROLL 15
(see p. 97)

On College, east of Bathurst
All-day breakfast, the real greasy
spoon experience. Open daily
from 7 a.m.

"When a muffin or a scone won't do."

Thobors
STROLL 16
(see p. 100)

Mitzi's Café
STROLL 17
(see p. 106)

Good Fork
STROLL 18
(see p. 114)

On Mount Pleasant
Tiny and cute, delicious croque-monsieur. Open from 7:30 a.m. (closed Mondays and Tuesdays).

Whimsical on Sorauren
So colourful, makes you happy! Open from 7:30 a.m. on weekdays and 9 a.m. on weekends.

On Bloor W., east of Jane
Loved second floor with large windows, and Eggs Benedict. Open daily from 9 a.m.

Coffee Tree Roastery
STROLL 18
(see p. 114)

Patachou
STROLL 19
(see p. 118)

The Beet
STROLL 20
(see p. 126)

On Bloor W., east of Jane
French toast, breakfast burritos... Open 7 a.m. to 7 p.m. (10 a.m. to 5 p.m. on Sundays).

"Ze real ting" on Yonge
Perfect croissants! Closed on Sundays, open other days from 8:30 a.m.

At Dundas W. & Medland
Quaint place, great patio Open weekdays from 8 a.m. and 10 a.m. on weekends.

Pain Perdu
STROLL 21
(see p. 130)

CocoaLatte
STROLL 21
(see p. 132)

King's Diner
STROLL 24
(see p. 150)

On St. Clair W., east of Rushton
Tiny, but everything is so good! So French! Open daily from 8 a.m. to 6 p.m.

On St. Clair W., east of Christie
Surprisingly vast breakfast menu. Open daily from 9 a.m. (10 a.m. on Sundays).

In Upper Beaches
Classic family restaurant, cute mezzanine. Open weekdays at 11 a.m., weekends at 8 a.m.

"Most restaurants listed in this guide also offer a brunch menu on the weekends."

Do you want to find a stroll around a great place
for a casual lunch?

BQM
STROLL 2
(see p. 19)

Burgers on Ossington
Cool decor, great side mural
Open daily from 12 noon to at
least 11 p.m.

Petit Four
STROLL 3
(see p. 24)

Catering counter on the PATH
Dessert shots, salad in a cup
Open weekdays 7:30 a.m. to 8
p.m. (Fridays, closes at 3 p.m.).

Marché Restaurant
STROLL 3
(see p. 25)

In splendid Brookfield Place
*Original food stations and all
kinds of rooms.* Open daily from
7:30 a.m. to at least 11 p.m.

Café Neon
STROLL 5
(see p. 34)

Close to West Toronto Railpath
Great light meals and coffee
Open weekdays at 7:30 a.m.
(10 a.m. on weekends).

Whippoorwill Tavern
STROLL 5
(see p. 38)

At Bloor W. & Lansdowne
Cool brunch place. Brunch
offered Friday 11 a.m. to 3 p.m.
and 10 a.m. to 3 p.m. on weekends.

Tatsu's Bakery
STROLL 6
(see p. 44)

Comfort food in Etobicoke
Great burgers with a twist.
Open 8 a.m. to 5:30 p.m. (9 a.m.
on Saturdays, closed Sundays).

Crêpe à GoGo
STROLL 11
(see p. 74)

French crêpes in Yorkville
*Sweet or salty, c'est très bon! Try
their own bottled lemonade.*
Open daily from 11 a.m. to 5 p.m.

Riverdale Perk Café
STROLL 13
(see p. 82)

The genuine local café
It's all good, sweet or salty!
Open weekdays at 7 a.m. and at
8 a.m. on weekends.

Sneaky Dee's
STROLL 15
(see p. 97)

At College & Bathurst
Food for bad girls...
Open from 11 a.m. on weekdays
and from 9 a.m. on weekends.

"Think good old carbs!
But there are other options too..."

Fish Store & Sandwiches
STROLL 15
(see p. 98)

The Little Dog
STROLL 15
(see p. 98)

Hey!
STROLL 17
(see p. 110)

On College, west of Grace
Best fish sandwich in town!
Open from 11 a.m. to at least 8
p.m. Closed on Sundays.

Behind The Big Chill on College
*Whimsical food counter with
large patio.* Open from 11:30
a.m. to at least 11 p.m.

On Roncesvalles
Lovely split level space
Open daily from 9 a.m. until at
least 9 p.m.

Baka Gallery Café
STROLL 18
(see p. 115)

17 Steps
STROLL 18
(see p. 116)

Rebel House
STROLL 19
(see p. 118)

At Bloor W. & Beresford
Very friendly, very yummy!
Opens at 8 a.m. Monday to Sat-
urday and at 9 a.m. on Sundays.

Walk 17 steps down!
Tapas menu and more. Lunch 11:30
a.m. Thursday & Friday, weekend
brunch 10 a.m. (closed Mondays).

At Yonge & Roxborough
Great pub food and ambiance
Open weekdays at 11:30 a.m.
and at 10:30 a.m. on weekends.

To Go Foodbar
STROLL 19
(see p. 121)

Cool Hand of a Girl
STROLL 20
(see p. 124)

Rawliscious
STROLL 23
(see p. 145)

At Yonge & Shaftesbury
Love the view! Good salads.
Weekdays 7 a.m. to 4:30 p.m.
(at least 9 to 2 on weekends).

Dundas W., east of Keele
Delicious sandwiches and more
Open weekdays 8 a.m. to 4 p.m.
(opens at 9 a.m. on weekends).

Near High Park on Bloor W.
*Yes, all raw! Intriguing and
tasty! You've got to try it once.*
Open daily at 11 a.m.

Note that we don't have a symbol for dinner, only lunch.
"Many of these also offer a dinner menu, call to confirm."

Do you want to find a stroll around a good place
for a fancy lunch?

Union
STROLL 2
(see p. 20)

Aria Ristorante
STROLL 3
(see p. 25)

Zocalo
STROLL 5
(see p. 38)

On Ossington
Heard food & patio are the best!
Open Wednesday to Saturday at
12 noon, Sunday at 11 a.m.

Near Air Canada Centre
Exquisite decor, great food
Open weekdays at 11:30 a.m.
and Saturdays at 5 p.m.

On Bloor W., east of Dundas
Everyone raving about the food
Open daily at 10 a.m. for cof-
fee, kitchen opens at 11 a.m.

Old Mill Afternoon Tea
STROLL 10
(see p. 67)

Pizzeria Libretto
STROLL 13
(see p. 84)

Glow
STROLL 14
(see p. 92)

Part of Old Mill Inn
Beautiful food and courtyard
Starts weekdays at 3 p.m., Satur-
days 2 p.m., Sundays 3:30 p.m.

At Danforth and Carlaw
Great urban decor, unique pizza
Open daily from 11:30 a.m. (tiny
patio, cool basement room).

In Shops at Don Mills
Trendy decor, great presentation
Open weekdays at 11 a.m. and at
10:30 a.m. on weekends.

DT Bistro
STROLL 15
(see p. 96)

Grano
STROLL 16
(see p. 104)

The Rushton
STROLL 21
(see p. 130)

On Harbord at Brunswick
Everything beautiful!
Open Wednesday to Sunday
from 10 a.m. to at least 10 p.m.

On Yonge, south of Manor
Unique patio, whimsical space
Open weekdays from 11 a.m.
and from 5 p.m. on Saturdays.

At Bloor W. and Rushton
Chic decor, tempting menu
Open Monday to Saturday at
11:30 a.m., 5 p.m. on Sundays.

Note that some restaurants close after lunch to get set up for dinner.
"For ladies who lunch (it's cheaper than dinner)."

Do you want to find a stroll around a good place
for (late) afternoon drinks?

Bellwoods Brewery
STROLL 2
(see p. 20)

On Ossington
Large patio in gorgeous space
Open weekdays at 5 p.m. and
at 2 p.m. on weekends.

Home Smith Bar
STROLL 10
(see p. 64)

Part of Old Mill Inn
Old English feel, comfy chairs
Open weekdays at 3 p.m. and
at 2 p.m. on weekends.

Allen's
STROLL 13
(see p. 86)

On Danforth near Broadview
Fabulous patio with huge trees
Open weekdays at 11:30 a.m.
and 10:30 a.m. on weekends.

The Boulevard Café
STROLL 15
(see p. 96)

At Harbord and Borden
Inviting patio with lovely mural
Open for lunch, closes at 4:30
p.m., then reopens for dinner.

No One Writes to the Colonel
STROLL 15
(see p. 98)

On College west of Bathurst
Great decor from the 70s
Open at 5:30 p.m. (maybe
earlier in the summer...)

Fat Cat Wine Bar
STROLL 17
(see p. 108)

On Roncesvalles
Backyard patio is a gem
Open Monday to Saturday at 5 p.m.

Baka Gallery Café
STROLL 18
(see p. 115)

Lovely decor at Beresford
Very friendly, very yummy!
Opens at 8 a.m. Monday to Sat-
urday and at 9 a.m. on Sundays.

Terroni
STROLL 19
(see p. 122)

At Yonge and Price
Rooftop patio, very cool decor
Open daily at 11:30 a.m. (go directly
to the slick second floor).

El Rincón
STROLL 21
(see p. 132)

On St. Clair W., west of Bathurst
Colourful backyard patio
Open weekdays at 5 p.m. and at
12 noon on weekends.

Note that many places stretch the patio season with heaters.
"Nothing feels like a holiday like having a drink on a patio!"

Author's favourite
TOP-3 **STROLLS**

Near Dundas W. & Bloor W.
(yes, they meet at some point!)

WEST TORONTO
RAILPATH STROLL
STROLL 5 **(see p. 33)**

Why?
For the four ambitious public art displays to admire + one original urban trail + waffles and coffee

North of Cabbagetown, east of Yonge

ROSEDALE VALLEY
FALL COLOURS STROLL
STROLL 11 **(see p. 69)**

Why?
For the unique urban valley road + best-kept-secret **Wellesley Park** (also great in the summer)

North of High Park

THE JUNCTION
SOULFUL STROLL
STROLL 20 **(see p. 123)**

Why?
For the focus on French industrial vintage + labour-of-love shops + cool restaurants

"I love all my strolls, for different reasons, but if you twisted my arm to choose, I'd go for these three."

TOP-3 STROLLS
for shopping therapy

West of Trinity-Bellwoods Park, between Queen W. & Dundas W.

OSSINGTON
EFFERVESCENT VIBE STROLL
STROLL 2 (see p. 15)

Why?
For the cluster of vintage and second-hand designer clothing stores + beer on the patio of **Bellwoods Brewery**

SUMMERHILL
UPTOWN GIRLS STROLL
STROLL 19 (see p. 117)

Why?
For all the home decor boutiques
+ gourmet food shops
+ **Terroni**'s great interior design

On Yonge, between Rosedale and Summerhill Subway Stations

THE JUNCTION
SOULFUL STROLL
STROLL 20 (see p. 123)

Why?
For all the well curated vintage furniture stores + unique shops + the **Junction Flea Market**

North of High Park

"These walks are great for window shopping and ideal if you're hunting for a statement piece."

Leave-it-all-behind
TOP-3 **STROLLS**

At the foot of Kipling (no, you're not in Mississauga yet)

ETOBICOKE
LAKESHORE STROLL
STROLL 6 **(see p. 39)**

Why?
For the ocean feel when the water is glistening under the sun + treats at **Tatsu's Bread**

Northwest of Bloor W. & S. Kingsway

OLD MILL
RIVER STROLL
STROLL 10 **(see p. 63)**

Why?
For the sound of the water running over the dams + café & croissants at **Ma Maison**

North of The Beach, east of Glen Manor Drive

UPPER BEACHES
STEEP STROLL
STROLL 24 **(see p. 147)**

Why?
For the wilderness trail nestled in the ravine + the national park feel, thanks to the new staircase

"Feeling grumpy? Your "hard-drive" is full? Maybe it's time to leave it all behind for a couple of hours."

TOP-3 **STROLLS**
with a street smart edge

Between Spadina and Christie

BLOOR WEST
COOL STROLL
STROLL 1 **(see p. 9)**

Why?
For the groovy second-
hand music and book
stores + landmark
Honest Ed's

Between Bloor W. & Carlton

SHERBOURNE
HIGH & LOW MIX STROLL
STROLL 4 **(see p. 27)**

Why?
For the contrast between the
empty streets around slick
condos on one side and the
bustling innercity life on the
other + **Allan Gardens**

Near Dundas W. & Bloor W.
(yes, they meet at some point!)

WEST TORONTO
RAILPATH STROLL
STROLL 5 **(see p. 33)**

Why?
For all the ambitious
public art displays to
admire + some original
out-of-the-way stores
+ an urban trail

**"The fun of living in a big city is all the street art
popping out in an everchanging urban mix."**

TOP-3 **STROLLS**
for movie buffs

South of Eglinton, east of Yonge

MOUNT PLEASANT
INDULGING STROLL
STROLL 16 **(see p. 99)**

Why?
Thobor's French pastries + Sunday matinee in one of the two independent theatres **Mount Pleasant** and **Regent**

Between Dundas W. & Queen W.

RONCESVALLES
REVAMPED STROLL
STROLL 17 **(see p. 105)**

Why?
For the line-up of shops, cafés and small restaurants to explore before the movie + independent movie theatre **Revue Cinema**

Between S. Kingsway & Kennedy

RUNNYMEDE
CASUAL STROLL
STROLL 18 **(see p. 111)**

Why?
Humber Cinemas + beautiful **Chapters** in old theatre + vast choice of restaurants (check **Earth Bloor West** with a roof-top patio)

"These strolls offer great dinner-and-a-movie combos, with a nice walk as a bonus."

TOP-3 **STROLLS**
for a romantic **outing**

OSSINGTON
EFFERVESCENT VIBE STROLL
STROLL 2 **(see p. 15)**

Why?
Best evening walk with the
street bathed in the warm glow
of the businesses + the line-up
of great restaurants

Between Dundas W. & Queen W.

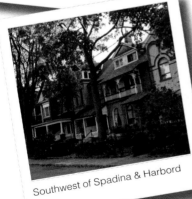

HIGH PARK
CHERRY BLOSSOM STROLL
STROLL 8 **(see p. 51)**

Why?
Gorgeous natural setting
(bonus if you catch the trees
in full bloom) + more secluded
section along the pond

Southwest of Bloor W. & Keele

HARBORD VILLAGE
DOLCE VITA STROLL
STROLL 15 **(see p. 93)**

Why?
Lovely walk in quaint
neighbourhood + beautiful
dessert at TD Bistro
+ drinks on a patio
(try **The Boulevard Café**
or **Tati Bistro**)

Southwest of Spadina & Harbord

**"Want to go out with your loved one?
Or on a first date? Try these romantic walks."**

TOP-3 **STROLLS**
to show off Toronto

Between Nelville Park Blvd. & Coxwell

THE BEACH
SOOTHING STROLL
STROLL 12 **(see p. 75)**

Why?
Sparkly **Lake Ontario**
+ long boardwalk
+ a dip into Toronto's
loveliest neighbourhood

Between Queen W. & Dundas W.

RONCESVALLES
REVAMPED STROLL
STROLL 17 **(see p. 105)**

Why?
One of Toronto's most
animated neighbourhoods
+ a cool mix of shops, cafés
and restaurants + bonus if you
can catch the **Polish Festival**
(mid-September)

Southwest of Bloor W. & Spadina

CASA LOMA
STAIRCASE STROLL
STROLL 22 **(see p. 135)**

Why?
Toronto's landmark castle
+ urban ravines (warning:
threat of property envy)

**"When you have visitors in town...
and they've already seen the CN Tower."**

Can't-believe-this-is-Toronto
TOP-3 **STROLLS**

Northeast of Yonge & St. Clair W.

MOUNT PLEASANT
CEMETERY STROLL
STROLL 9 **(see p. 57)**

Why?
For the Old English
country feel
+ the amazing variety
of trees

North of Cabbagetown, east
of Yonge

ROSEDALE VALLEY
FALL COLOURS STROLL
STROLL 11 **(see p. 69)**

Why?
For the kind of landscape we
only see in movies + French
crêpes at **Crêpes à GoGo**

Southwest of St. Clair W.
& Bathurst

WYCHWOOD
COUNTRY STROLL
STROLL 21 **(see p. 129)**

Why?
For a true oasis in the
middle of the city + good
little restaurants nearby

**"Sometimes, when strolling around the city, you just
can't believe you're in Toronto!"**

TOP-3 **STROLLS**
for winter days

Between Major & Christie Streets

BLOOR WEST
COOL STROLL
STROLL 1 **(see p. 9)**

Why?
Fun second-hand stores
to explore thoroughly
+ play-all-day games at
café **Snakes and Lattes**

Southwest of Dundas & Yonge

PATH
UNDERGROUND STROLL
STROLL 3 **(see p. 21)**

Why?
Great corporate architecture
from within + intriguing indoor
public art + hot chocolate at
Foodwares + near **Nathan
Phillips Square Rink**

Southeast of Queen E. & Coxwell

THE BEACH
SOOTHING STROLL
STROLL 12 **(see p. 75)**

Why?
For the blue and grey hues
of the beach under the
winter sun + Christmas
lights along the boardwalk
around Balsam Avenue

**"Most of the walks are better during other seasons but
these strolls would do a good job during the winter."**

TOP-3 **STROLLS**
to explore with kids

Southwest of Dundas & Yonge

PATH
UNDERGROUND
STROLL
STROLL 3 **(see p. 21)**

Why?
Tunnels everywhere
+ great playground for a
treasure hunt (looking for
the signs) + snacks at
Foodwares

SHERBOURNE
HIGH & LOW MIX STROLL
STROLL 4 **(see p. 27)**

Why?
Upside-down wolves
+ **Allan Gardens'** giant dogs
+ **Chew Chew's Diner**
with train mural

Between Bloor W. & Carlton

CASA LOMA
STAIRCASE STROLL
STROLL 22 **(see p. 135)**

Why?
Toronto's castle to admire
+ **Baldwin Steps** to climb
+ wetlands to explore

Southwest of Bloor W. & Spadina

**"These strolls should fire up your kids' imagination.
They won't even notice they're walking!"**

ICAL INDEX

ALPHABETICAL INDEX

ALPHABETICAL INDEX

Chocolates

Churches

Coffee shops

D

E

ALPHABETICAL INDEX

G

ALPHABETICAL INDEX

P

Q

ALPHABETICAL INDEX

Restaurants

T

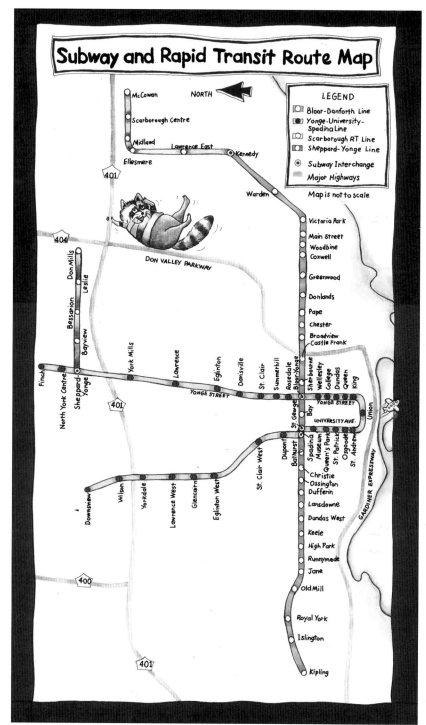

Strolls by subway stations

Want to go carless? Here's a list of Toronto subway stations included in the strolls featured in this guide.

Bathurst Station
Included in **Stroll 1**

Bloor Station
Included in **Stroll 11**

Broadview Station
Included in **Stroll 13**

Chester Station
Included in **Stroll 13**

Christie Station
Included in **Stroll 1**

Davisville Station
Included in **Stroll 16**

Dundas Station
Included in **Stroll 3**

Dundas West Station
Included in **Stroll 5**
and **Stroll 17**

Dupont Station
Included in **Stroll 22**

High Park Station
Included in **Stroll 8**
and in **Stroll 23**

Jane Station Station
Included in **Stroll 18**

Keele Station
Included in **Stroll 8**

King Station
Included in **Stroll 3**

Lansdowne Station
Included in **Stroll 5**

Old Mill Station
Included in **Stroll 10**

Spectacular *Cross Section* by **William McElcheran** (northwest entrance to Dundas Station).

Queen Station
Included in **Stroll 3**

Rosedale Station
Included in **Stroll 19**

Runnymede Station
Included in **Stroll 18**

Sherbourne Station
Included in **Stroll 4**
and **Stroll 11** (a good option only if the Mount Pleasant staircase is open)

Spadina Station
Included in **Stroll 1**

St. Andrew Station
Included in **Stroll 3**

St. Clair Station
Included in **Stroll 9**

St. Clair West Station
Included in **Stroll 7**,
12-min walk from
Stroll 21 and **Stroll 22**

Summerhill Station
Included in **Stroll 19**

Union Station
Included in **Stroll 3**

Make this combo work for you!

Leave **Toronto Fun Places** with your family while you take off for a few hours to enjoy Toronto with your girlfriends, **Toronto Urban Strolls** in hand. Everybody wins!

Sold in the **Travel** section of major bookstores, or online at: **www.torontofunplaces.com**

Because **happy mom = happy family**
(or is it the other way around?)